TO Mickey,

My Best Wishes

5/4/03.

What Shall I Do Next
When I Don't Know Next What To Do?

Special Edition

Praise for

What Shall I Do Next When I Don't Know Next What To Do?

"Co-hosting with Dr. Willie on the set of Singsation has not only been a fascinating adjunct to my on-camera career, but a true inspiration to my personal life as well. His book is sure to bless everyone who reads it!" *Merri Dee, Directior, Community Relations, WGN-Television*

Truly, this book is a lesson in reality and should be considered a masterpiece endorsed by God. *Rev. Harold E. Bailey   President, Pincham Probation Challenge Chicago, IL 60628*

"What Shall I Do Next" is a refreshing and positive book that speaks to the champion within. Dr. Wilson's fascinating journey encourages us to move undauntingly towards our dreams even in the face of insurmounable odds. *Effie   Rolfe   Gospel   Radio   Personality   Newspaper   Columnist*

This book is about believing, about loving one another, about forgiveness, and finding peace in Jesus Christ." *Review by Chinta Strausberg, former political reporter for the Chicago Defender Newspaper and host of the PCC's "Strausberg Report."*

WHAT SHALL I DO NEXT

WHEN I DON'T KNOW NEXT WHAT TO DO ?

The Extraordinary Story of a Man, His Faith,
and the Building of a Financial Empire

This edition published by Willie Wilson Productions, Inc.
Willie Wilson Productions, Inc., P.O. Box 129,
Matteson,IL 60443

What Shall I Do Next When I Don't Know Next What To Do?

Unless otherwise noted, all Bible Scriptures are taken from the King James Version

First Edition

Book design by Jonathan Clark
Cover and Bio photos by Brian Wiles

ISBN 978-1-4363-5045-7

To my parents,

Douglas and Lula Wilson

ACKNOWLEDGEMENTS

To my Rock; my Salvation; my Lord:
Thank You for Your Word. Your Word is a lamp unto my feet and a light
for my path. It is by Your Word that I have the wonderful privilege to
share with others and live abundantly.

To my wonderful wife, Janette:
Thank you for your remarkable strength, encouragement and support.
You are truly my ideal help-meet.

To the memory of my beloved Father:
His amazing strength taught me to stay strong during trials and
tribulations. I miss him and I bless God for the many years He gave us
together on this earth.

To my dear Mother:
Thank you for your love, firm discipline, kind heart and incredible
support. I thank God for allowing me to be your son.

To my sister, Dale:
I appreciate your existence in my life more than you'll ever know.
Thank you for being my friend, as well as my right hand and
confidant in business.

To McGhee Williams-Osse:
Had it not been for your persistent urging for me to tell my story, this
book would still just be a thought. I appreciate you bugging me about it
– it was all worth it.
To all who have helped in the production of this book, particularly

Anna Morris, Jonathan Clark, Kathy Russell and Terri Stingley:
What can I say but, "THANK YOU, THANK YOU AND THANK YOU. No matter how small a part anyone may think they played, it was huge in terms of bringing this book alive.

To The Wall Street Journal Staff Reporter, Dorothy Gaither:
I wish to publicly thank you for the flattering article you wrote on me in your newspaper. That article actually laid the groundwork for the emergence of this book.

To Rev. and Mrs. McKinney:
Thank you for imparting in me the uncompromised Word of God, and for your encouragement down through the years.

To the hundreds of pastors, teachers and community leaders who I call "friend:"
I am in awe of your energy and strength to do what you do for God's people. Thank you for letting me assist in your journeys.

To my children, family members, friends and business colleagues in the US and abroad:
Thank you for enriching my life in so many unique ways.
May God richly bless you all.

Last but not least, to anyone who has ever asked the question,
"What shall I do next?"
I applaud you, for marching forward in faith, anyhow,
"when you didn't know next what to do."

WHAT SHALL I DO NEXT

WHEN I DON'T KNOW NEXT WHAT TO DO?

Contents

INTRODUCTION

15

Part I
FROM COTTON TO CHICAGO
19

Part II
IN THE SHADOW OF THE ARCHES
39

Part III
COMING INTO MY OWN
51

Part IV
WHEN TITHES ARE NOT ENOUGH
69

Part V
WALKING A NEW ROAD
85

FOREWORD

Dr. Willie Wilson is classic proof that faith, boldness and commitment can produce incredible success and wealth. It was that faith and boldness, along with the willingness to do whatever it takes, that empowered him to approach Ray Kroc, Chairman of McDonald's Corp, in 1979, with big dreams and no money, and ask for a McDonald's restaurant. My favorite book says, "Ask and it shall be given unto you; seek and ye shall find; knock and it shall be opened unto you." When this young, but eager Wilson went asking, seeking and knocking, in an effort to sell Mr. Kroc on his idea, not only did Mr. Kroc give him a restaurant, but he also arranged for a bank to loan him the necessary $50,000 seed money. The rest, as they say, is history.

On each page of Dr. Wilson's book – brilliantly encased in the stories of his monumental struggles, obstacles and misfortunes – are practical and strategic nuggets of wisdom that show you how his financial empire was built. It takes you from his humble beginnings of picking cotton; to his days of sweeping floors and flipping burgers; to owning five McDonald's restaurants; as well as a long-running, syndicated entertainment program; and now a global distribution company, with offices in Shanghai and Beijing, China. This story proves that Dr. Wilson is actually not an exception, but rather an example of what hard work, integrity and commitment can bring to *a n y o n e* who wants to succeed in life. I applaud Dr. Willie Wilson for not only achieving all that he envisioned and more, but for reaching back with his philanthropic efforts, making it possible for others to "get theirs" as well.

Les Brown

Les Brown is a World Renowned Motivational Speaker and Author.

It is easier for a camel to go through the eye of a needle, than for a rich man to enter into the kingdom of God.

Mark 10:25

INTRODUCTION

Now go, write it before them in a table, and note it in a book,that it may be for the time to come for ever and ever.
Isaiah 30:8

My name is Willie Lee Wilson, and I do not want to go to Hell. I had a sufficient taste of it in the cotton and cane fields of Louisiana. I want to go to Heaven, but Heaven is not guaranteed. Yet, it is a promise through Jesus Christ, who paid for our salvation. It is up to us to accept his gift. Living a Christian life, sharing my wealth and bringing God's Word to as many people as I can is my way of giving back to the one who has given me everything. It is my way of saying, "Thank you." Through many trials and tests, God has blessed me abundantly, and now I am a rich man trying to work his way through the eye of the needle.

I started to write this book more than once, but my busy life would get in the way, or the time didn't feel right. So I waited. Now I have embarked on a business venture that is so momentous, and so historic, that I know that the right time has come. I want to take you along on my continuous journey from cotton fields to corporate conference rooms; from 20 cents an hour to millions in annual sales, from poverty to philanthropy, and from fear to faith.

My life is proof that, despite disappointments, dreams can come true. I left home at thirteen. I was stranded and penniless in New York when I was a teen-ager. I've been jobless in Chicago. I have lost loved ones. I have lost money. I have faced prostate cancer. And I have prospered.

Throughout my life, I have encountered obstacles that seemed insurmountable and I've run into my share of dead ends. Many, many times I found myself at a crossroad, not knowing which way to turn. Time after time, like you, I have asked the question, "What shall I do next?" I hope that by reading my story you will discover, as I did, that the answer is simple: work hard, keep the faith, trust in Jesus and you will know next what to do.

Now the things, which I write unto you,
behold, before God, I lie not.
Galatians 1:20

There's an old saying that if you can't say anything good about a person, don't say anything at all. I try to live by that, but this is my story and I have to include certain incidents and involve certain people. Unfortunately, the situations aren't always good. I can't leave them out, because these situations or incidents shaped my life and who I am, even if I don't have anything good to say about the people in them. My compromise is not to name names. That way, if you don't know who I'm talking about, it won't matter. The bottom line is that names or not, everything you read here is the truth. I cannot talk about Christ and tell lies in the same book.

Willie Lee Wilson

PART I

FROM COTTON TO CHICAGO

It is good for a man that he bear the yoke in his youth.
Lamentations 3:27

Right now, I am on my way to China on business. As I breathe in the recycled air of the First Class cabin and look out the window, I can't help but reflect that the Lord has brought me a mighty long way from Gilbert, Louisiana, where I drew my first breath on June 16, 1948. I was born in a shotgun house, so called because you can shoot a gun through it without hitting a wall. Anybody with a good arm can stand in the front door and throw a rock all the way though it and out the back door. It was the typical living quarters for sharecroppers like my daddy, Douglas Wilson.

Webster's Dictionary defines sharecropper as "a tenant farmer especially in the southern United States who is provided with credit for seed, tools, living quarters, and food, who works the land, and who receives an agreed share of the value of the crop minus charges." In reality, sharecropper translates into black and dirt poor. Maybe it's different in other places, but down south, before Civil Rights laws and the emergence of the "New South," sharecropping was just a baby step up from slavery.

Tenant farmers like my daddy rarely came out ahead by sharecropping. Everything that Daddy needed to work the farm had to come out of our share of the "profits," and they were never a fifty-fifty split. The white man owned everything, including the cabin we lived in. He even owned the store that supplied anything we couldn't grow, and he kept a running tally of all our purchases and acquisitions, including the denim for our overalls, all our medicines, Mama's frying pan, and that precious piece of penny candy. The white man also did all the bookkeeping. If a year was extremely good, and we had worked extremely hard, we might clear enough for new shoes and a "little something to put back." If it was a bad year, there was nothing but more debt to show for a season of hard work.

Our "shared" crop was cotton. My family supplied the backbreaking labor of plowing, planting and picking, and the white man got the lion and tiger's share of the proceeds. All of us worked in the fields, even the children. I literally grew up there, and I don't recall that carefree childhood "poor" kids have in the movies. In fact, one of my earliest memories is picking cotton when I was about four years old. I would put my little mite in my mama's sack and when I got tired, I would crawl on top of it and go to sleep. She would pull me along as she worked her way down the row.

My mama, Lula Mae Wilson, never stopped working. She was typical of rural southern black women of that era. She married at sixteen and started having babies. Lots of babies. I was the third son, behind Caleb Douglas and Henry Lee. After me came my brother, Charles Earl, a still-born sister and another sister, Gloria Dean. These were the brothers and sisters that I knew best. They were followed by another brother, Ricky, and five more sisters: Dale, Deloris, Sarah, Penny and Lisa. In all, eleven little Wilsons made it to adulthood. My mama considered us blessings, my father thought of us as needed hands, and they both knew we were more mouths to feed.

My mama's life was defined by children, church, cooking, cleaning, and cotton. Her old-fashioned, cast iron stove

With my mama, daddy and three of my brothers. I'm the one in the suspenders.

burned wood. Her dishwasher came with two black hands. Diapers were not disposable. She made our clothes. She boiled her sheets in a huge pot set over a fire in the yard, and she scrubbed our shirts and overalls by hand. She was faithful to God and Douglas Wilson. By any measure, she was a good woman.

My daddy was a good man, too. I think he was born in Wisner, which is about nine miles from Gilbert. Before I brought him to Chicago, he never travelled further than nine miles in any direction. He had to take his hat off when he talked to a white man. He had to avert his eyes from white women, and step off the sidewalk to let a white child pass by. Sometimes I reflect on that when I take my seat in the forward cabin of an airplane and smile at the blonde flight attendant. The Lord has surely brought me a mighty long way.

Daddy was a sharecropper like his father before him, living hand to mouth. He couldn't afford to spend "quality time" with his children because his every waking minute was devoted to our survival, and that meant working seven days a week. Most days, he would be in the fields with us. At sundown, when the rest of us went home, he headed off to do other work around the plantation and he might not get home until after midnight. There were times when he didn't get home until two or three in the morning, and we had to be up by six. Once in a while he would join us when we went to the little wooden church where we worshipped the Lord. Then, more often than not, he would have more work to do somewhere on the property. There was always something—repairing fences, digging trenches, shoeing horses and anything else the white man needed. In between time, he parented. In other words, he whupped our behinds when we stepped out of line.

Sunday was the one day we didn't automatically go to work in the fields. On free Sundays, we went to church and learned about Christ and the Christian life. On those rare occasions when we could afford it, we would go to the picture show in town, but we had to sit up in the balcony because the main floor was "for whites only." I would sit up there mesmerized by cops, robbers, cowboys, war movies and Tarzan. The white man was always the hero and anybody that looked like us played the fool.

When we got the chance, my brothers and I would use our free time to go bird hunting or fishing for something to put on the table. We never actually went hungry because there was always bread, syrup and some kind of greens, but meat was something rare and wonderful. So coming home empty-handed was a sorrowful thing. Hunting was actually dangerous because we were trespassing and poaching, and it was most dangerous at night. My mama's heart was in her mouth every time any of us boys went off on one of our expeditions, but of course, we never thought of the danger. We were young and thought we were immortal.

I'm sure we caused my mama to have many heart-stopping moments. We were boys, after all. On top of that, we were black boys in the pre-civil rights south, and there's an extra element of parental concern wrapped up in that. Aside from teaching us to say "yes'm" and "nossuh", and to obey God and anybody "grown," my parents had to drill into us the ironclad Rules of Behavior Around White Folks: Step off the sidewalk if you see them coming down the street; don't look white folks in the eye, and, "for Gawd's sake, don't you ever get too friendly with no white woman!"

That last lesson was forcefully brought home to me when I was about eight years old. On our way to school we had to pass a house with two white girls who were very friendly. Anytime we passed, they would smile and wave. "Hi, niggers," they would call out. We knew better than to respond. One day, two of our school mates forgot the rules. They smiled back, they waved and they went inside the house. I don't know what they did inside. It doesn't matter. They should never have crossed the threshold. Now, there's always somebody ready to tell on you. This time it was a neighbor, a black man, who called the police. "There some black boys inside them white girls' house."

The police dragged them out of the house and onto the street. A crowd gathered but nothing happened for some time. The police were waiting for a man named Jimmy Guice. Jimmy was known for beating up niggers. He was the enforcer. Nobody touched them until Jimmy got there. Time dragged on and the black population was gathered on one side of the street so they could bear witness to the lesson of the day. When Jimmy arrived, they started beating and preaching. "See this? See this? You uppity niggers better pay attention." The boys' father had to stand and watch, as helpless as the rest of us, while Jimmy and the police beat those boys bloody with their fists and billy clubs, and stomped them with their feet. Then they hauled them off to jail in Winnsboro.

They released the boys the next day and let their father take them home. In a few days, the family left town and nobody heard from them again. The rumor went around that they went to California. Curiously, the same time that they disappeared, somebody got into Jimmy Guice's house and shot him dead. Nobody ever found out who did it.

We lived in a time and place where the color of your skin made a big difference in how you could behave and how you were treated, and it worked on your head. I knew a black boy named Bubba, with skin that was magnolia white, and everybody knew who his father was. It wasn't the black man that was out in the fields chopping cotton with us everyday while the white man parked his truck in front of Bubba's house. Everybody knew, but nobody would say anything because there was nothing anybody could do, not if they wanted to keep on living. That kind of thing robs you of your dignity and self respect, but it happened all the time. It was part of the landscape.

It was situations like this that made me want to get as far away from Gilbert as fast as I could. It is not easy to overcome poverty, but it is much easier to mend the hole in your pocket than the hole in your spirit.

**Your young men shall see visions
and your old men shall dream dreams.**
Acts 2:17

The first time I left home, I was only thirteen. I made my way to Thibodaux, which is only about nine miles from Gilbert. I thought I could do better in the cane fields. I was so wrong. If my nightmare is picking cotton for a white man under a hot Louisiana sky, my idea of hell is cutting cane for the white man under a hot Louisiana sky. In fact, when they burned the stalks in the field, the smoke and the fumes made me think I was already in that bad place. It didn't take long for me to decide that this wasn't where I wanted to be, either. I worked there for one season and went back home.

By the time I turned sixteen, we were working on a farm that paid us 20 cents an hour. It wasn't much, but it was steady, and we got our money at the end of the day. We survived, but we were still struggling. I was still young, but I already knew this was not the life I wanted for myself. I didn't want to spend the rest of my days working on a white man's farm. My dream was to make a better life for my mother and father before they passed away, but at 20 cents an hour, I couldn't take care of myself, let alone try to raise a family or do anything for my parents. So I made the decision to leave. Again.

Caleb, my oldest brother, was the first to go. I wasn't far behind him. My daddy didn't want either one of us to leave home, particularly me. Farming was all he knew, and he didn't think a sixteen-year-old boy had a chance out on his own. Mama didn't want me to go, either. She always said I was headstrong, and I proved it by telling her I was going to go, anyway. So she relented. "Let him go," she told my father. "Otherwise, he'll wind up stuck behind a mule, and picking cotton just like us. Nobody ever got nothing down here. Our parents didn't get nothing, and he won't either if he stays here. He'll wind up having babies and working for the white man. So let him go. "

I took with me the clothes on my back and my mama's parting advice to remember the things I had been taught: honesty, integrity, respect and reverence for the Lord. At first, she said, "Watch out for white people," but then she changed it to "We're Christians. Judge people by the way they treat you. Whatever you do, don't hate anybody because of the color of their skin." I never forgot that. My mama and my faith tell me that I must love everyone, whether I like it or not.

I have been a stranger in a strange land.
Exodus 2:22

I knew there was nothing for me in Gilbert. So when they came through recruiting migrant workers, I quickly volunteered. Along with other recruits, I boarded a worn-out yellow bus bound for Delray Beach, Florida. There were forty-two of us on board, all from the Gilbert, Winnsboro, Thibodaux area. I was the youngest in the group, but the oldest boy was only about 19. We were all homeboys with high hopes.

This was the first time I had ever been this far away from home, and I was fascinated. Crossing the state line was pretty exciting stuff for a country boy that had never been more than nine miles in any direction. I had visions of returning home loaded with money. I didn't know I had traded one form of servitude for another.

The layout of the farm they brought us to reminded me of the plantation in Gilbert. There was a "big house" for the boss and a dilapidated area on the back of the property for us field hands.

We were housed and fed every day, but we didn't realize that our bunks and beans constituted "room and board" that would be deducted from our meager pay. They put us to work picking butterbeans and tomatoes. It wasn't easy, but I didn't think it measured up to chopping cotton or cutting cane. After three months, the work stopped. We sat around with nothing to do except play basketball and increase our indebtedness. When we finally worked up the nerve to approach the boss and ask about our back pay, he made it very clear that there was no such thing. Our living expenses had eaten it all up. When we asked about getting more work to pay everything off, he explained that the best we could ever do would be to break even, and leaving was out of the question. I finally realized I was still in slavery.

I am escaped with the skin of my teeth.
Job 19:20

As the unproductive days passed, we became more desperate. We couldn't leave the camp in Delray Beach, because we had nowhere to go. We had no idea what next to do until one of the guys slipped away and returned with news about opportunities further south, along the coast. He said that if we could just get away on a certain night, there would be another bus to transport us there. All forty-two of us decided to leave, but that was easier said than done. We couldn't just walk out the front gate. Our boss had made it very clear that we were virtual prisoners. So we plotted an escape. We passed the word around that we were going to sneak out in the dead of night, but somehow the white man found out. Well, of course he did. Somebody told him.

It was like a movie. The night was dark, the moon was bright and we were expected. Mean dogs and meaner rednecks, armed with shotguns, were blocking the direct route to the highway. Praise God, it was raining.

We ran until we came to a wide pond that ran the length of the plantation. It was only about thirteen feet wide, but the other side seemed like it was an ocean away. All the guys jumped across. All, except me. I was the youngest and smallest one in the group, and I couldn't swim. Everybody was on the other side, waiting for me to come over. I looked at that water and thought of alligators. I looked behind me and thought about dogs. I waited until the last minute. Then, I took a running start. In the movies, my adrenaline would have miraculously carried me across to the other side. That's not what happened. I fell short, but the other fellows pulled me out, soaking, shivering and scared as hell. The dogs and the guns stayed on the other side, and we started running for the highway. Our pursuers loaded the dogs into their cars and headed toward the highway, too. They intended to cut us off that way.

At one point, we hid under a viaduct, and my heart stopped when our pursuers stopped almost directly above us. I guess the water we were squatting in masked our scent. I don't know if they were too tired or too drunk. In any case, they gave up and went away. We climbed out of the viaduct and started running. And running. I was the youngest, but that night, I was the fastest. I don't know exactly how far we ran, but it felt like we had to run forever before we reached the highway. Sure enough, the school bus was waiting to transport us to Mexico Beach, Florida; to pick tomatoes.

As we headed south along US 95, we passed by Miami. I liked the look of the city. It was the biggest one I had seen so far, and I made up my mind to go back. After all, I was down there to make it so I could take care of my parents, and picking tomatoes was not the way to riches.

Even so, this work camp was an improvement over the one in Delray Beach. This time we got paid. By the day. We worked for two days, picking tomatoes and butterbeans, making $1.00 an hour. I saved my money, but most of the guys spent theirs on whiskey, cards and, of course, women. At the end of the second day, I decided to go back to Miami and seek my fortune. I think I had about $14 in my pocket.

I shared my intentions with Robert and a boy we called "Fat," my closest friends in the group. At first they were skeptical, "What you going to Miami for? You don't know anybody there. Where you going to get a job? " "I don't know," I replied. "But I'm going and I'll find something. It's got to be better than here." My confidence must have rubbed off on them because they decided to go with me. I didn't mind Robert and Fat tagging along; they still had most of their money, and they could pay their own way. I warned them not to tell anybody else, but they let it slip to one or two, and word got around to everybody. Naturally, the other guys wanted to go, too. I tried to explain that they needed money for bus tickets, food and a place to stay, but they weren't hearing it. They wanted to come with us, and that was that.

Since we slept in a huge dormitory, it was difficult to do anything in secret. We couldn't sneak away. When we got up the next morning, the others got up with us. From then on it was like a desperate game of Hide and Seek. They started shadowing us. We tried to ditch them when we went to buy our bus tickets, but they stuck to us like Krazy Glue™. When it came time to catch the bus, we started running. And they chased us, begging us not to leave them behind. Some were even crying. It was an awful thing.

They chased us all the way to the bus. The bus driver asked if he should wait, but we urged him to "go on, go on!" He rolled out and left those thirty-nine young men in the dust. I didn't feel good about it, but I didn't think I had a choice.

The Miami bus station was close to the railway yards. Since we didn't have any particular destination, we started walking past all these old trains until we came to an open field. Some distance ahead, I saw an old man picking up cans and putting them into a sack. He didn't look like a derelict, so I approached him as politely as I could. "Sir, we're looking for jobs. Can you help us find work?" "Why, yes," he replied. "Go that way, son." He pointed to the end of the field. "Turn right, go five blocks and you can get all the work you want." We got so excited we broke into a run. Then I realized that I hadn't thanked him. I stopped and turned around, but the man was gone! We were in a space as big as a football field, with no obstructions or buildings that could conceal him, and we had only been running for about five seconds, but he was gone. I believe that old man was my first angel. I believed in angels back then because my momma told me they existed. I believe in them now because I have been touched by more than one.

His directions brought us to the beach and jobs. We got hired on as beach boys, making about $25 a week. That was good money back in those days. We didn't even have to buy our food, because we were working for restaurants and cafes. So now we had our beach cards with a picture ID, our nifty little uniforms and a decent salary, but we needed someplace to stay. We couldn't sleep on the beach.

Our new boss helped us out by sending us to some Negro-friendly accommodations on the west side of Miami. The three of us rented one room in the Imperial Hotel at 850 NW 8th St. Today, the area is multicultural, and the hotel has been replaced by a strip mall, but back then we were in a mostly black neighborhood. The area around the hotel was okay, but down on Second Avenue you could find panhandler's, prostitutes and pot, any time of the day or night. For a while, we stuck to the television in the hotel lobby.

My mind was still on the thirty-nine guys back on the work farm. I must have looked down, because my boss asked me what was bothering me. So I told him about the boys we left behind and how we were all from the same area. I asked if he could find them jobs, too. My boss said, "Wilson, you're a good worker. So I tell you what. I'll hire some of them and I'll call all my friends. We'll get every one of them a job. You take time off and go get them, tomorrow." I was excited. I told Robert and 'Fat' and we went back to Mexico Beach, Florida, and I bought –bus tickets for the whole group. I paid for them out of my own pocket. At the hotel, I asked the desk clerk for some more rooms because there were forty-two of us in all. The desk clerk was from New Orleans, so he was inclined to help his homeboys, but he would only give us one more room. "You'll have to take turns." Then he turned to me, "Wilson, I'm going to hold one person responsible for the rent, and that's you."

To make a long story short, they worked one day . Then they quit. Every single one of them quit. They also left the hotel and the bill. I was embarrassed because my white boss had gone out of his way to help them, and they didn't work out. He told me that he knew that was going to happen, but I never saw it coming.

I was stuck with the rent for both rooms, so I went looking for them after work. I found them down on Second and Third avenue, drinking, gambling and whoring. It shocked me because that's not how we were raised. We didn't know anything about that kind of carrying on. At least I didn't, but I was young, naïve and a mass of raging hormones.

I was brought low, and He helped me.
Psalms 116:6

Now, down on Miami's Second and Third Avenues, they had a thing called 2-2-2: $2 for the prostitute, $2 for the room, and $2 for the pimp. I was only sixteen, far from home and my mama's eyes were not on me. I was ripe for sin. So one night, I took my six dollars over to Second Avenue and found myself a willing woman.

Horny as I was, though, I didn't tear off her clothes, or mine, immediately. Instead, something moved me to ask her why she had turned to prostitution. Her answer stuck with me for a long time and was the beginning of my realization that you can't always judge a book by its cover. She told me that prostitution provided for her children. She wanted them to have a better life than she did. She came from a welfare home, had no education and no training for anything else. She said, "I sell my body so that I can buy food for my kids." There was nothing I could say to that.

Since that night I have often reflected on the reasons that people may do the things they do, and I try not to jump to hasty conclusions, or to condemn people out of hand. People in different conditions make decisions for a variety of reasons. If a thief steals food because he is hungry, who can blame him? Who knows what we might do in the same circumstances? I know I would. The thought of that prostitute's sacrifice fills me with compassion to this day, but it did not stop my sixteen-year-old self from "doing the do."

I soon discovered that my six dollars had bought me a dose of VD, but I didn't know what it was. All I knew was that I was sick, and I went to the doctor. I wasn't aware that in Miami you couldn't work for six months if you had VD, particularly on Miami Beach. I didn't know enough to lie. So my boss took away my beach card and fired me.

Now I didn't have enough money to eat or pay rent, and none of my home boys on the street would help me out. Not one of them would give me a dollar. When I asked Howard and Fat to help me just for a month, Fat said, "No, but I will give you money for a one-way ticket back to Gilbert." That's the last thing I wanted. I did not want to go back home with my tail between my legs, but I had no alternative. Fat bought me that one-way ticket and put me on the bus.

My return to Gilbert was not joyful. My mama was disappointed to see me come back, because she really wanted me to escape that life. "Why on earth," she wanted to know, "would you come back here?" I didn't have an answer for her because I was too embarrassed and ashamed to tell her why I lost my job.

My friends were a drag on my spirit, too. "Well, well, well. Wilson's back home. He couldn't make it." To make matters worse, my best friend had started going with my girlfriend.

After gagging on the bitter pill of my homecoming, I told my mother that I was going back to Miami. I didn't know what I was going to do, but I knew I wanted to get away from Gilbert. If I was going to fail, I preferred to do it in a city where nobody knew me. Mama suggested going to Chicago. I didn't want to do that. I wanted to go to California to be with my brother, Caleb. Mama insisted. "I have a sister in Chicago," she said. "You could stay with her and since you're in such a hurry to get away, you could go up there with cousin Buster. He's leaving tomorrow." "Buster" Tilman was a second cousin with a car. His other passenger was a lady who had been my second-grade school teacher.

Mama was determined. "C'mon, Willie. Just try it and if you don't like it, we'll pay your way back to Miami." What did I have to lose? Anything was better than staying in Gilbert.

Rejoice, O young man, in thy youth.
Ecclesiastes 11:9

I fell in love with Chicago, but not at first glance. At first glance, I was scared of it.

Since the school teacher was going on to Detroit, Cousin Buster drove us downtown to the Greyhound bus station on Randolph Street. The teacher got out and said her goodbyes. I stayed in the car. "Well," Buster said. "You're in Chicago." I still didn't get it. "I live in Wheaton. This is as far as you go," he told me, as he opened the door and nodded toward the sidewalk.

Up to this point, the biggest city I had ever visited was Miami, but the Miami of the 60's was a low-rise city. Chicago was skyscraper tall, and I was still a country boy— a teen-aged country boy. So there I was, alone on Randolph St., surrounded by these monstrous buildings and scared to death. I had one dollar, one dime and my auntie's phone number on a piece of paper in my pocket. I had never used a public telephone in my life, but I remembered what I saw in the movies and on television. So I put my thin little dime in the slot and dialed the number on the piece of paper. Luckily for me, my aunt had taken the day off and was home to answer.

Aunt Elizabeth and her husband, J.T., came downtown, picked me up and took me to their home. I stayed with them for nine months, and Uncle J.T. got me a job at a piano factory in Melrose Park, on an assembly line making piano parts. I really, really didn't like it. So I quit.

My auntie didn't receive this news very well at all. "Boy, you don't quit no job without another job in your pocket. You're not gonna lay up in here with nothing to do. If you don't have a job, you have got to go."

So I moved out of there and into a one bedroom apartment on the west side. My first cousin, Leo, moved in with me. He had come to Chicago a few months after I did. He was my best friend. We were closer than brothers and remained that way until the day he died.

Even though I had made it up in my mind that I didn't want to work anymore, Leo and I had to eat and we had rent to pay. So we started painting apartments. We actually made a lot of money. On paper. Nobody would pay us. I think we were too young for anybody to take us seriously, and we certainly didn't know anything about contracts and stuff like that. Between our non-paying jobs, we drove around and learned the city.

Eventually, I went to work at the Goldblatt Tire Center. Then at Goodyear, fixing flats, but I decided that I'd rather be a hustler. I don't know how I got it in my head that I didn't want to work, anymore. I certainly wasn't raised that way.

By this time, my oldest brother had joined me and Leo, and the three of us hit the streets. We didn't get involved in anything shady, but we got into all the things idle minds and hands can find. We'd stay out all night long and go straight to work in the morning. Sometimes we would sleep in our clothes, "ready roll." We were having a wonderful time. I had my own car, a '64 Oldsmobile. I was eighteen and I thought I was hot stuff.

Hanging out in the clubs, I met this guy who said he was a doctor in a family of doctors. Now, I'm from the South and we southerners tend to believe what you tell us. We take you at your word, because you can trust ours. So when my new friend, Robert- the-doctor, said he needed to get to New York, but he didn't have the money to get there, I said, "Come on, let's go. I'll drive."

When we got to the Big Apple, we checked into the William Sloane House YMCA, down the street from Madison Square Garden. The room was a little box, just large enough for a bed and a nightstand, with a washroom down the hall. There was nothing to do in the Y that night, so we went to a little club near the Garden. Right away, we met two ladies from Baton Rouge, Louisiana. Naturally, we paired off. I asked the lady I was with, "Where are you living?" "Oh, we're not living anywhere. We don't have any money." Quite naturally, I went in my pocket and gave them all the money that I had, around $6. Remember, that was good money back in those days. The lady I was with said, "I owe you something for this money." "No, you don't owe me anything. You're from my neck of the woods. You keep this money and do what you need to do." I had learned my lesson about strange women and my mama raised me to be a gentleman. Besides, I figured Robert would reimburse me in the morning.

Young Willie on the move

The next morning, I looked out of my tiny room window and discovered my car had been towed. That's when my friend confessed that he had no money. He had lied about being a doctor, and he didn't have a doctor brother or doctor sister. Then he left without paying his bill. So there I was. Penniless, no car, stuck with the room rent and hungry.

This was the first time in my life that I had to call home for money. My parents wired me $15. And I know they had to borrow it from the white man.

I felt so bad I went out and found three jobs in one day. And I worked them all, putting tiles in ceilings, fixing truck tires at BF Goodrich and parking cars for the movie stars at 20th Century Fox. I started working that very evening, went back to the hotel to pay my rent and was back on the job that same night. I worked round the clock for about a week, but I had to sleep sometime. So I quit the job at BF Goodrich. The best job was parking those cars. I made some good tips, which is a good thing because my car was still in the pound, ringing up

$5 a day, plus the $50 for towing. I had to work for three months before I could get it out and park it in the garage where I worked.

New York was too fast for me and I was anxious to get back to Chicago, but when I told my boss I was planning to leave he asked me to stay. He told me he liked me. I thought he meant I was a good worker, but then he put his hand on me in a way that didn't feel right at all. I didn't know anything about "gay," but I knew I didn't want any of what he was offering. So I quit right then and there, walked downstairs, got in my car, cranked it up and drove non-stop back to the west side of Chicago.

When I got back to the Windy City, I think I had about $2.50 in my pocket. The gas and tolls had eaten up my ready cash, and it was like life started over again for me. I was right back where I started: I still hadn't done what I left home to do; my parents were still in slavery. I was drawing unemployment and running wild. I never got into anything criminal and I wasn't into drugs, alcohol or cigarettes, but I loved ladies, cards and dice. I gave up my apartment on the west side and moved in with Robert Slack, a Louisiana friend who lived on the far south side with his mother, Carrie Lloyd.

Finally, I decided to move to California and live with my brother out there. But Carrie suggested going to work for the McDonald's close to her job. I didn't really want a job, but I figured I could work at McDonald's for a few weeks, draw my unemployment until it ran out and then go to California. It didn't work out that way.

PART II

IN THE
SHADOW OF
THE ARCHES

Whatsoever thy hand findeth to do, do it with thy might.
Ecclesiastes 9:10

I got a job in the McDonald's at 170th and Halsted, flipping burgers and picking up litter in the parking lot. There weren't any other black employees, and hardly any ever came in as customers. Needless to say, I wasn't very popular with my co-workers.

After I had been there a few weeks, all the managers walked out. I was actually getting ready to quit myself, but my boss asked me to stay. I was the only adult who knew any of the procedures. So out of desperation, he offered me a job in management. I told him that I was leaving, but he insisted. I stayed because I sort of liked the idea of wearing a Crew Chief's shirt and tie. The minute I put them on, the problems started. The crew kids gave me as much grief as they could because they didn't want to work for a black man. Some quit and I had to fire others that slacked off on the job. They didn't know it, but if they had left me alone, I would have left on my own. But when they started hassling me, I decided to stay. I was determined not to let them run me away, no matter how hard they tried. And try they did. They shot out my car windows and they threatened my life. It was hell. I would call the police, but they wouldn't come because they didn't want me there, either. I had a white security guard, but he was only for show. He certainly wasn't on my side.

It all came to a head one night when a huge gang of kids- and their parents - surrounded the store, making threats and a lot of noise. There must have been three hundred people outside. It was a mob, with a mob's mentality. I should have been scared, but at some point, you go beyond fear, straight to mad. I had reached that point. Like Rosa Parks, I was tired. So I "armed" myself by putting two empty toilet paper rolls in my pockets, and I went outside to confront them. In the dark, it must have looked like I was packing serious "heat."

"I'm tired of this now," I said. " So if you want me, come and get me. But I promise you, somebody is going to die." They responded with a logical question. "How are you going to fight all of us?"

"Well," I said. " I know I can't kill all of you, but I can get some of you. I can probably get at least five." I put my hand in my pocket and turned to the big mouth in the front. I got right in his face. "I'm going to start with you. You will surely die tonight. I'm through talking."

With that, the ones in front backed away and parents started dragging their children out of the parking lot. I can imagine what they thought. "This black man is crazy enough to try to kill us all." They probably used the "N" word because they had no trouble using it to my face.

That night ended the threats, the vandalism and the harassment. From then on, I didn't have any more trouble with any of the crew or the customers. Some of them even tried to become friends with me.

The laborer is worthy of his reward.
I Timothy 5:18

I met Roland Jones when I was working at that first McDonald's job. Back then, he was a Field Consultant for the corporation, and he was always looking for ways to increase black participation in the system. Later, he would become a charter member of the NBMOA (National Black McDonald's Operators Association). After observing me for a while, he recommended that they promote me to manager. This was definitely a step up for me, but it required skills that I didn't have. Yet.

I may not have a college education, but I have mother wit, common sense and the will to succeed. It's a good thing, because I had to learn the McDonald's system on my own. There was no Hamburger University for me, no training program and no mentor. The white shift managers had come back to work, but they weren't inclined to welcome me into their group or make anything easier for me. So I would stay in the office by myself at night, looking over the books, trying to puzzle out what the other managers did and why they did it. I kept at it until I had the system and procedures down pat.

I worked five years straight without a day off. That may sound incredible, but it's true. I was prepared for it. Just like marathon runners who can go long distances because they train for it, picking cotton in Louisiana and tomatoes in Florida made me accustomed to hard work. I had a field hand's endurance, and I could go from sunup to sundown, day in and day out, doing whatever had to be done. I needed a field hand's endurance because I had a wife and four children to support.

One day, it occurred to me that I should ask for a raise. I was dependable, I was responsible and I worked non-stop. I had trained the white crew and the white managers. I thought I deserved some kind of monetary recognition and the chance to manage one of his other stores. He had eight, and I trained the managers in all of them. I thought that deserved some kind of consideration. My boss evidently disagreed with me because he fired me.   Actually, he sent his nephew to fire me.

I asked, "Lord, what do I do now?" I had a wife, four kids, no job and no savings. My wife didn't take the news very well. "I'm taking the kids," she said. "And I'm going to my mother's." "Wait, wait, wait. You know I'm a provider. I'm a hard worker. We'll make it some kind of way." "You always say that. We've been married five years and we got four babies. We don't go nowhere, we don't do nothing. You work all the time. You don't ever spend any time with us. I don't even have a car to go to the store." I jumped on that. "I tell you what. We'll go get you a car, right now." I went to the dealer, lied and said I was still working, and signed for a car. She was so glad to get it that she didn't waste any time loading the kids into it, along with all their clothes and her personal belongings. "I'm going back to my mother," she said. " And you can take your black ass back down south and get behind a mule where you belong."

I had come to another dead end. I had worked seven days a week for five years and I didn't have a dime to show for it. My mama and daddy were still down south, and my wife and children were gone. "Lord, Lord, sweet Lord. What do I do now?" I felt so down I was sick with it. I started getting pains in my chest, and I thought I was having a heart attack. In the emergency room, they told me it was just anxiety after running up a big bill I couldn't pay. I was worried, sleepless and hurting. All I had left was prayer.

Well, like it says in Psalm 30:5, "weeping may endure for the night, but joy cometh in the morning." The very next day I got eighteen job offers from McDonald's owners around the country. I picked one in Chicago. It happened to belong to McDonald's first black franchisee.

By the time I went to work for him, my new boss owned two stores and he was no longer the only black McDonald's franchisee. There was a growing number of black entrepreneurs who had seized the opportunity to walk through the franchise door he had wedged open. In 1972, they had formed the NBMOA. At first, it was more or less a support group where members would trade helpful information and horror stories. In time, it would become a powerful lobby within the McDonald's system, but not back then.

A lot of the NBMOA members owned more than one store, and this was an inspiration to me. I told my boss that my plan was to work for him for a few years and then get my own McDonald's. I wish I could say that I was encouraged. The truth is the opposite. I don't know if they felt they were saving me from heartache and disappointment, or what, but none of the other black operators ever said, "Yeah, Wilson. That's a good idea." They never invited me to join their exclusive club.

And so now, I was working for a black man and I couldn't do less for him than I did for the white man. So I managed one of his stores and I trained his other managers. I worked non-stop, for five more years. It came to a halt after an eventful Sunday that started at home.

It is better to dwell in a corner of the housetop,
than with a brawling woman in a wide house.
Proverbs 21:9

You know how it is, when you break up to make up. Well, my first wife and I had gotten back together and things were a little better. We weren't in a one-bedroom apartment anymore. We had a little home out in Hazel Crest, she had a car and I gave her money every week. However, she still griped about my hours, and she had a definite problem with our miserable financial situation.

This particular Sunday, I picked up my Bible to go to church and I was walking out the door when my daughter asked me to bring her some milk. I said, "Why don't you just get some milk out of the icebox?" Her mother said, "That milk is for the baby."

That didn't sound right. "Wait a minute, didn't I give you money for groceries?" She didn't say anything so I told my daughter to just go on and get herself a glass of milk. That made her mother mad, so when I turned to walk out the door, that woman hit me on the back of my head with the clothes iron. I hit her back. Not with the clothes iron, with my fist. This was the first and last time in my life that I have ever laid a hand on a woman. I'm not proud of it, but I did it. It was a reflex action. Judging from her reaction, I must have hit her hard. "You better run, you son of a bitch! I'm calling the police!" I started to get in my car and leave, but I've never run from anything. So I stayed to face the music.

We were living in Hazel Crest, not back on the west side, so the police response was immediate and in force. There must have been a dozen squad cars. Our neighbors came out in force, too. While they watched, two of the officers went into the house to talk to my ex-wife and two more had me up against the wall. They wanted to know what happened. "Did you hit her?" I confessed that I had. "I'm not a wife beater, but I did hit her. I don't deny it." When they asked how it happened, I explained about the iron and they could see the blood on my head.

One of them said, "I wish I could get away with hitting my wife one time." They all looked at each other. Then, miraculously, they let me off. "Look," they said. "Get in your car and leave. Give your wife time to cool off. Don't come back, tonight. And don't make us sorry we gave you a break." They didn't have to tell me twice. I got in my car and headed into Chicago. I was due back in the store, but I wound up at the Marriott downtown, instead.

With Baby Kenya.

I was drowning my sorrows in the hotel lounge when I struck up a conversation with a lady who was going through her own domestic problems. One thing led to another and we wound up comforting each other all night. I was embarrassed because I didn't have money to pay for the hotel room, and ashamed because I had strayed. I was feeling bad about being a wife beater and cheater in the same day.

Things didn't get any better when I made it to work. It was Monday morning and everybody was in a management meeting. When I walked in, my boss lit into me. "Where were you yesterday?" I apologized for my absence and I tried to explain that I had some personal problems and couldn't make it in." My boss wouldn't hear it, and he kept ragging on me, "Dammit, Wilson. If you can't make it in, maybe you need to work someplace else." That didn't seem fair because I had never taken a day off. So I got mad, too. We had words and I used as many ugly ones as I could think of as I told him what he could do with his job.

Instead of walking out, I locked myself in my office for three hours and reflected. Here I was at another crossroad. My marriage was in a shambles, my job was over and my mama and daddy were still down south in slavery. "Now what do I do?" In my mind, a quiet voice whispered, "Call Ray Kroc."

Ask, and it shall be given unto you; Seek and ye shall find; Knock and it shall be opened unto you.
Matthew 7:7

Ray Kroc, founder and CEO of McDonald's Corporation, was the man who made it the most successful fast food system in the world. He was at the top of the McDonald's pinnacle and I was somewhere close to the bottom. It took me a while to get up the nerve to call him. When I did, his secretary, a serious gatekeeper, didn't think much of my credentials. Desperation made me persistent and she finally made an appointment for me to see Mr. Kroc, but not right away. When I found out there was a shareholders' meeting in Oak Brook sooner than my appointment, I made it my business to attend.

As you can imagine, he was surrounded by a lot of white folks who wanted "just a moment" of his time. I stubbornly worked my way to the head of the line and shook his hand. "Mr. Kroc," I said. "I want a store. I have nothing to offer but my integrity and my willingness to work hard." These were two qualities that he valued very highly. There are stories that he would drive up to a McDonald's in his limo, get out and pick up litter in the parking lot. There are also many stories about his kindness and generosity. I believe them all.

As he shook my hand, he said, "I want to talk to you. Meet me over at my office." I told him I had an appointment for such and such a date, but he said, "No, I mean right now." I thought he would want to wait until after he talked to all the waiting people, but he said I was the most important person in the place. "You mean more to me than anybody here. Come on. Let's go." With that, he turned his back on the other people and left the auditorium. He headed for his office with me right behind him.

We talked for a long time and I gave him my background. I think he was sensitive to me because he didn't finish high school, either, and he was no stranger to hard work. He was also the nicest human being I ever met in my life, and the only reason I got my first franchise. The black

McDonald's operators certainly didn't want me to get one. In fact, they fought the idea. They even tried to convince the regional manager, Jack O'Leary, not to let me have a store. Ray Kroc was just the opposite. After our talk, he took me across the street to a cocktail reception where he introduced me to the Licensing Manager and told him to give me a store. Just like that, it was done.

The first store they offered me was in San Diego, but Jack O'Leary knew that I wanted to be in Chicago, so he put a proposal together for a Chicago store. Mr. Kroc agreed. His primary concern was for me to get a store, regardless of the location.

Now my problem was seed money. Thanks to Mr. Kroc, the six-figure franchise fee was not an issue, but I still needed cash for operating expenses that first year. Fortunately, my friend Jim Fletcher was an officer of South Shore Bank, and they loaned me the $50,000.

I didn't have much contact with Ray Kroc after that. I would see him at conventions, but we didn't talk. I had one more conversation with him when they celebrated his 80th birthday out in San Diego. I took my turn and went to shake his hand. He surprised me by remembering me and he kept me by him to chat a while, as the line of well-wishers grumbled behind me. That was the last time I saw him alive.

PART III

COMING

INTO

MY OWN

Blessed shall be thy basket and thy store.
Deuteronomy 28:5

It didn't take me long to discover that there's a world of difference between running a business and owning a business. For one thing, your headaches and your ulcers are way larger. When a shift is over, managers can walk away. If the stress becomes too much, a manager can quit. An owner has to tough it out, no matter how bad it gets. Managers have headaches, but owners have the risks, the accountability and the ulcers. If an employee gets injured on the job, it's the owner's responsibility to have the proper insurance. An owner has the liability: if something happens to a customer, it's the owner's problem, not the manager's. If the sales are bad, an owner still has to pay the taxes, carry the debt and meet the payroll. In the case of a franchise, it's the owner that has to make sure that the total operation is in compliance with the franchise agreement.

Learning the McDonald's system from an owner's perspective was another challenge. Fortunately, I had an angel named Reggie Webb in my corner. Reggie was a Director of Operations for McDonald's and he made it his business to give newcomers assistance above and beyond the call. He guided me through the intricacies of my franchise ownership, giving me tips, shortcuts, advice and a strong shoulder to lean on. He shared information that helped me profit by other people's mistakes and avoid serious mistakes of my own.

**And through his policy also, he shall cause
craft to prosper in his hand.**
Daniel 8:25

Becoming "the man" did not mean that now I could sit back, relax and delegate. I knew I couldn't do that if I wanted to succeed. So I worked as hard for myself as I ever had for my former bosses, and I made sacrifices. I was making less than $30,000 a year, but I took a 30% decrease in pay and forced myself to live within my reduced means. I was divorced with four kids, but I made that money stretch to cover all my needs and obligations. I had common sense enough to know that I couldn't go into the cash register at the end of the day, count up my cash and put it in my pocket. I wouldn't spend an extra penny or give myself a raise until I knew all the factors that came into play.

I knew a lot about running a store, but there was a lot that I didn't know about the business of business, about profit and loss projections, taxes and all the other things that can trip up a new entrepreneur. So I got an accountant, and I listened to his advice. I also listened to the advice of anybody and everybody in the system. I went to every meeting and conference that talked about ways and means.

In the process of listening, I had to weigh what I was hearing. Just because most of the people in the system were white, I couldn't jump to the conclusion that what they were saying to me was racist. By the same token, I couldn't trust everything that black people told me. So it came down to using my judgment and dealing with what was said, not who said it.

I also sweated out the kind of long hours, sixteen or seventeen a day, that my new venture required. I had to put aside all my personal concerns and focus solely on the business. I couldn't let anything distract me from it. This was the hardest choice that I had to make. I figured that if I took care of the business, the business would take care of my family. Every entrepreneur faces this choice: family first or business first? A "life" now or success later?

It all boils down to hard work and sacrifice. So if you're contemplating an entrepreneurial venture, my advice is to work hard, listen well, judge wisely and be willing to sacrifice your personal life.

The hard work and sacrifice paid off for me. I ran my first store so well that when another owner ran into problems with his store, McDonald's called on me to take over for him. His store was run down and he was losing money. I took over and doubled the receipts within a year. I wound up with four stores in two and a half years.

My sister, Penny, working at my Madison Street restaurant.

**When I was a child, I spake as a child, I understood as a child,
I thought as a child: but when I became a man,
I put away childish things.**
I Corinthians 13:11

One thing about fast-food operations is the age of the employees. They are mostly teenagers, and when you have teen-aged employees, you're not just a boss, you're a stand-in parent, too. I spent as much time trying to keep my crew kids in school as I did trying to keep them on the job. It was the first job for some of them, so along with their on-the-job training, we taught the kids some basic stuff like how to fill out an application, how to dress, how to comb their hair and how to get along with people. Even if customers work your nerves, you have to be courteous and respectful. Teenagers have a hard time with that. Fortunately, McDonald's has a lot of internal programs for their crew kids. We could give them flexible hours and, sometimes, tutors. We also had "rap" sessions where they could air their problems and talk over solutions. Sometimes those problems were pretty heavy.

The average McDonald's crew kid is only sixteen. In the depressed areas where I had my stores, some of my crew kids were already parents, single parents with three to five kids. Most of them lived difficult lives. One young lady had been raped three times. The first time was less than a block from the store, right on the sidewalk in sight of pedestrians who walked past without stopping or interfering. The second time, she was snatched from the bus stop, thrown into a van, driven to an alley, gang raped and then dumped in the street like trash. I think she was three or four months pregnant at the time. The third time, I told her she didn't need to be coming to work on the west side. It hurt my heart that I couldn't do anything more than adjust her hours, but we couldn't work out any other solution. This kind of problem came with the territory.

And above all things have fervent charity among yourselves.
for charity shall cover the multitude of sins.
I Peter 4:8)

My new role as a McDonald's owner meant that I had to become more involved with the community, because that's McDonald's way. If you own a McDonald's, you have to be a good neighbor. This is particularly true, if you have a store in the "hood." You can't just

take money out of the community without putting something back in. If you have a successful store in a depressed area, everybody comes at you for money, including people off the street. I got involved in a lot of community organizations, including daycare centers, boys and girls clubs, nursing homes, churches, little league teams, you name it. I can't think of a community organization I didn't support because I tried to help everyone I could. If someone approached me and asked for something to eat, I'd give it to them. I might ask them to pick up the litter in the parking lot in exchange, but I wouldn't let them go hungry.

Fortunately, I'm a people person, because McDonald's is definitely a people business. You have to become actively involved with your employees, your customers, the community and your company. It wasn't always sunshine and roses, but it was always spiritually and emotionally rewarding.

For thou, Lord, art good, and ready to forgive; and plenteous in mercy unto all them that call upon thee.
Psalms 86:5

Be careful how you treat people because you never know when you might need them. The man who sent his nephew to fire me when I asked for a raise had to come to me for help. Come to think of it, he sent his wife to ask me. Close to ten years had gone by, and he had left the McDonald's system to join Burger King. He needed money to meet his payroll, and he asked me for something like $25,000. I guess he had forgotten the realities of our past association, because you would have thought I was his closest friend.

There might have been satisfaction in saying, "No!" I considered refusing, but Scripture made me reconsider. So I wrote him a check for $25,000. My sister, Dale, thought I was crazy and told me so. I explained to her that helping him was the right thing to do, regardless of how he had treated me.

Time passed and he got back in the black, but not back to me. I never heard from him and he never offered to repay me. I didn't forget, but it was never at the front of my mind. For some reason, I started thinking about it one day, and the whole situation made me mad. It wasn't the money, it was the principle of the thing: I wouldn't have minded it if they had not been in a position to repay me. I could have forgiven the debt without a second thought, but they just ignored me as if I owed them the money. I finally had to get my attorney to jog their memory, and they paid me back —without interest. That's way better than a bank loan.

They have rewarded me evil for good, and hatred for my love.
Psalms. 109:5

I don't believe in "shacking up." It would be hypocritical to say that I never have, but that was the old me, before I made my commitment to live my life for Christ. Even the old me didn't really want to do it and I never really liked it. It just happened and it had disastrous results that taught me a lesson.

I met the young lady, when we were both working at the same McDonald's. When I left to get my own franchise, she followed me over to my new store, although I originally told her to stay where she was. At the time, she had a long-term boyfriend that was an ex-convict. I believe he went to jail for killing somebody, but I'm not sure. That should have told me something about her, right there. Anyway, after I went through my divorce, we started to date.

I had just bought myself a home in Country Club Hills and she would spend weekends with me. Come Sunday night, she never wanted to go home because she was living with her mother and, according to her, they didn't get along. One weekend she announced that she'd had a big row with her mother and just couldn't face going back. So I gave in and she moved in.

By that time, I had three stores and was able to treat her pretty well. I wound up buying her three cars. I bought her a nice wardrobe, and we went on fabulous luxury vacations, flying first class and all that.

To keep things kind of fair, I asked her to help me out in one of my stores. That was another bad move. I have since learned not to mix emotion with business.

One day, I got a call from her best friend. "Willie, I need help," she said. My boyfriend and my baby and I are out in the cold. We don't have any place to stay."

"You really need to be calling your friend," I said. "Not me."

"I know, but she won't do anything. Please help me. I wouldn't ask if I wasn't desperate." Now it was mid-winter in Chicago, the temperature was on the mean side of zero, and I didn't feel good about the baby being out there in that freezing weather. So I met them on the corner of 79th and Ashland and gave them $3,000, to get a hotel room and some food. When she thanked me, I said "You have to promise never to tell your friend." Time passed and I didn't think any more about it.

One day, the phone rang in my office, and you know how you can get that feeling of wrongness? Well, that ringing just didn't feel right, and I did not want to want to lift that receiver. I let the phone ring as long as I could. It kept ringing, so I finally answered. It was my live-in's best friend, again. "I just wanted to let you know that your lady is downstairs," she said, "in her mother's house. She's having sex with another man. I wouldn't be telling you this if you hadn't helped me out. I been telling her she shouldn't do this because you're a good man." Then she told me the make, model and license number of his car.

I put the phone down and I forgot about my business. I forgot about my responsibilities. I forgot I was a "good man." I walked out of my store and drove to her mama's house. By the time I got there, I had cooled down a little, but not a whole lot.

Sure enough his car was sitting outside.

Her brother opened the door, and delayed me long enough for the outside man to make a getaway. I happened to look back over my shoulder as his car was pulling out. She came up out of the basement as if nothing was out of the ordinary. One look at my face and she could see that I was in no mood for ordinary. When I confronted her, she broke down and told me she was sorry. "But why would you do this?" I wanted to know. Her tearful response was, "You haven't spent enough time with me. It just happened. I'm so sorry. Will you forgive me?" Well, I had to wrestle with my faith. Scripture was telling me to forgive her. So Good Willie forgave her, but Bad Willie did not let it go.

Since she had hired her boyfriend's son as a crew kid in one of my stores, it was no problem getting his home phone number. I called his house. His wife answered, so I just left a message. "Tell him Willie Wilson wants him to call." It didn't take long for him to call me back. I told him when and where to meet me and I hung up the phone. I drove to our rendezvous point and waited. When he arrived, I waved him into my car and did all the talking. "Look man. I know all about you. I know about your wife, your ex-wife and your child support. But I don't want to know you. I don't ever want to see you. If ever you see me come into any place where you are, you leave. End of conversation." But that was not the end of the story.

About a year later, I got another one of those calls. This time, I was told that my lady was at 79th and Wolcott with the same person. I didn't run down there this time. I just waited for her to get home. It was harder to forgive her this second time, but I did. However, I didn't forget it.

One night, while we were being intimate, I realized that I hadn't seen her taking her birth control pills every night as she normally did. I asked her about it. "Oh, I take them in the afternoon now." That sounded reasonable, so I forgot about it. That would come back to haunt me.

I got a call one last time. This time the woman in my life was in a hotel downtown. I was not in a forgiving mood when I got home. When I confronted her this time, there was no "I'm sorry." This time she said, "I'll do what the F—- I want to… and I want you to get out of my house."

That came out of nowhere. So I said, "Come again. Don't you mean my house?"

"No," said Miss Thang. "I mean my house."

"Is that right?" I asked. "How do you figure that?"

"Well, I've been living here and I've had my mail coming here for the last two years. That's grounds for Palimony. So it's my house."

"Oh, is that right? You've must have been reading stuff about Lee Marvin."

"Yeah," she said, looking around at the house. "This is mine."

She was smug until I asked her if she had consulted an attorney. "Or have you just been listening to your friends? Those laws only apply to the states of California and Oregon. The reason I know that is because I called my lawyer when you first moved in here. "

I confess I was angry, and I had a gun. That's a bad combination, so I unloaded the weapon before I waved it at her and escorted her out of "my house." Ironically, BB King supplied her exit music. They were playing the "The Thrill is Gone" on the radio.

It was a hard lesson, but it was good for me. I was able to forgive. I had matured.

Remember those birth control pills? Well, a month after we split, she took great pleasure in telling me that she was pregnant. Of course, I insisted on a blood test. The first one indicated that it was my child. So did the second one. So my attorney told me to go on and accept responsibility. It was a boy. For eighteen years, I sent support checks every month. I stopped when he decided not to go to college, but she demanded continued support. She claimed our son was mentally retarded and that I had to support him for the rest of his life. This was definitely not something I wanted to do. My attorney felt that she would settle out of court if I offered her a lump sum. His reasoning was that a settlement would cost less than the legal fees and the time I would have to take away from my stores. I didn't like it, but I decided to take my attorney's advice. I thought that was the end of it. I should have known better.

One day at church, I got a call from American Express. "Dr. Wilson, where do you want us to mail your new Gold Card. We have more than one address for you." "What Gold Card? Why should I get a Gold Card when I have a Platinum Card?" "Well, Dr. Wilson, we have your application here for a Gold Card. Do you live in Riverdale?"

I hired a private investigator and, in short order, I knew exactly who was stealing my identity. It was good old "you know who." This situation was threatening to mess up my credit, so I decided to press charges. This was back before Identity theft became the bugaboo it is today, so the local police weren't very interested in anything that wasn't life-threatening. As one officer said to me, "We don't have time for this. We have to worry about people getting killed." I finally had to pull some strings and call in some favors to get it all resolved. I haven't heard from either one of them since, but the boy still calls my sister, occasionally. I have forgiven them both, and I wish them well, but I don't want to have anything to do with anybody that would stoop to cheating me.

**And the Lord God said, It is not good that the man should be alone;
I will make him an help meet for him.**
Genesis 2:18

My first marriage started wrong and never got right. We met just after I started working at McDonald's. Almost immediately she got pregnant. I don't think either one of us was thinking about marriage, so she had an abortion. Then she got pregnant, again. This time we decided to make our union legal. It didn't work. We didn't have a solid spiritual foundation, so the pressure of finances crushed any hope of us ever making it.

I don't fault her because I did promise her things that I couldn't deliver. It was hard on her, and on me. I worked so much we never had any time to play. Even if I had found the time, we didn't have any money. That was always a problem, especially since we had four kids in five years.

Things got better after six years, but not much. By then we had a little house in Hazel Crest that was an improvement over our old one-bed-room apartment, but I still worked seven days a week. That didn't make my wife too happy. Our miserable financial condition was the biggest bone of contention. We argued about that a lot. Even so, we tried to hold it together for ten years, but we decided to split permanently about the time I got my first franchise.

I think that more than anything else, I was embarrassed and shamed by my inability to do things for and with my wife. It wore me down and I felt boxed in.

I don't know if it was only about money, because I look back at my parents. You can't get much poorer than they were, but their marriage was strong and it endured. Maybe if I had the faith back then that I have today, things might have been different, but this was at a time when my faith was low on the scale of one to ten.

With my beautiful wife, Janette

The second time around, I went about marriage the right way. Janette and I met in church, at the prayer altar. It wasn't the first time she was at my church, it was just the first time I noticed her. She was actually a member of long standing, all her life to be exact, but she always sat in the back, close to the door. When service was over, she would get up and leave. So I never saw her. When I did, her beautiful face was imprinted on my mind and I had to meet her.

We took our time and got to know one another. We had both been in marriages that weren't too happy, so neither one of us was in any hurry to go that route, again. After seven years, though, Janette said that we ought to at least think about it. We did for another three years. By that time, we knew we could make a go of it. My parents looked on her as another daughter, and her parents embraced me as a son. There was no "impediment," as they say, so we tied the knot and we are now in our second decade of marriage.

Obviously, it is easier this time because poverty isn't threatening to move in with us, and I have more time to devote to the relationship. One thing that my first wife always bitterly complained about was that I never had time for her. I never took her anywhere and we never did things as a couple. I guess romance had gone out of the marriage. I try to make sure I keep it in this time. During the week, we're both busy in our separate working worlds, but Friday night is always our "date night." We go out to dinner, movies, plays, concerts, or whatever else strikes our fancy. As Bill Withers' song says, "just the two of us." Then Saturday is another day for "togetherness" things which might include other people. Of course, on Sunday we worship together.

That's the main reason that it's better this second time around. We share spiritual values that make our union stronger. Janette takes an active part in my ministry and she's always in the front row when I'm in the pulpit. When there's money to be given, she presents the check, because I want her to have something to do besides sitting in the pew. In the true biblical sense, she is my helpmeet.

Another reason that it works is because we look at our marriage as a matter of give and take, and it's not about who wins an argument. On those occasions when we have a serious difference of opinion, we take it to the Lord in prayer. If we have a problem and we can't come to an understanding, we let go and let God. In my opinion, that's a much better approach than trying to split your spouse's head open with a clothes iron.

I don't think I'm a qualified marriage counselor, and every situation is different. However, my advice is not to expect your friends to be qualified counselors, either. Keep your in-laws out of your business, too. Treat your spouse with respect and talk to them the way you want them to talk to you. Most important of all, if you let go and let God, you should be okay.

PART IV

WHEN TITHES
ARE NOT ENOUGH

With my song will I praise Him.
Psalms 28:7

I cannot live the life that he has given me without giving back. It's not enough just to go to church on Sunday. I have to do more than sit in the pew. So I started praising him through song.

First, I tried singing in the choir, but that didn't work. Even though I love music, it hasn't always loved me, and the choir director didn't either. Still, I wanted to lift my voice in praise and, every once in a while, Reverend McKinney would let me sing a solo. He was a kind man and would tell the congregation, "Listen to the words, children. Listen to the words." I don't know what the congregation thought, but the choir director made his feelings obvious. Every time I got up to sing, he would get up from the piano bench and walk out. Every time.

In time, we came to an understanding. I offered to pay him to teach me some music and he gave me some instruction, but I think he begrudged every minute of it. He became my accompanist and stayed with me for a while after I put my band together.

We had our ups and downs because, to put it mildly, he was somewhat temperamental and he was a true test of my Christian principles. He would yell at me in rehearsals. He didn't care who was around. One time, he quit on me, complaining about his salary. I upped it, but he never stopped yelling.

He stayed with me until he got sick. He was so ill that he couldn't sit up on his own. He had a tumor and no insurance. So I paid for his medical treatment and cleared up all his debts. He was going through a divorce, so I took care of those expenses and his back child support. When he went into the hospital, I would visit when nobody else would, but we didn't grow any closer. I got another piano player.

We were out of touch for a long time. Then I found out one Sunday that he had gone back into the hospital. By the time I got home from church, I got a phone call that he had passed away. I prayed, "Lord, I thank you for the things that he has done, and if he has done anything that is not pleasing in your sight, I ask for your forgiveness on his behalf." My relationship with this man gave me ample opportunities to turn the other cheek. I will do so and forgive as often as Christ tells me, because I firmly believe that by following God's commandments, you earn a place in the Kingdom of God.

And if a house be divided against itself, that house cannot stand.
Mark 3:25

If you Google® the Norfleet Brothers, most of the articles will mention me, and the impression you'll get is that I was an important part of the well-known gospel group. Not so. Although I did make many appearances with the Norfleet Brothers, there was only one song they ever let me sing with them.

Our association began at Christ Temple Baptist Church. Arthur Norfleet was sitting next to me on one of those Sundays when I sang a solo, and received my normal bad reviews. We struck up a conversation and he told me that he would help me out with some lessons. I was ready, willing, eager and grateful as a puppy. For the next thirteen years, I stuck to the Norfleets like glue. I traveled with them, I rehearsed with them and they taught me one song. Since I was a successful McDonald's operator, I could afford to express my gratitude by picking up the tab for travel expenses and rehearsals. I did that a lot, and they let me sing my one song.

When we went to Chicago's Gospelfest, I would try to steer the media away from Willie Wilson of Singsation and toward the Norfleet Brothers, but no matter how much or how often they interviewed the group, the resulting article would say something like Willie Wilson and the Norfleet Brothers, just like you'd say Smokey Robinson and the Miracles, Gladys Knight and the Pips or James Brown and the Flames. As you can well imagine, this annoyed the Norfleets. I don't blame them, but I honestly did not try to hog the spotlight. I guess it looked that way to them and they got a little testy. Eventually, they got more than testy and when I went to rehearsal, most of the time was spent in complaints. I finally got tired of the animosity and that was the end of Willie Wilson and the Norfleet Brothers.

Sing unto the Lord, all the earth.
Psalms 96:1

Singsation, my television show, has been a part of my life for more than two decades, because I wanted a way to say "Thank You" to the Lord for all that he had done for me. I was sitting in church one Sunday and the choir started singing "What shall I render unto the Lord for all his benefits toward me?" I started thinking about how blessed I was, and I became uncomfortable. Sure, I tithed, but tithing wasn't enough. It's too easy to write a check once a week. I went to Sunday School and Bible Class, but that wasn't enough, either, and I felt I needed to do more than warm a bench every Sunday. So I started thinking about all the praise that is in music. I thought about the way music uplifts the soul, and that's when the idea of Singsation came to me. I decided to do a Gospel television show as a way to serve the Lord.

By this time, I had been with the Norfleet brothers for quite a while. We were regulars on Jubilee Showcase, a local Gospel show in Chicago. My style was much improved, and I was comfortable singing in public. So the thought of hosting a TV show didn't scare me, but I didn't know how to go about getting one on the air. At the moment, all I had was an idea and the determination to make it a reality.

The first thing I needed was a sample show, what they call a "pilot," to take around to the TV stations, but I knew nothing about putting one together. I had to learn the hard way, and my lessons were very expensive. My first producer took advantage of my ignorance and left me in a severe financial bind.

Things started out okay. I had a well-known gospel singer to co-host the show, several choirs and quartets were lined up and scheduled to perform. My producer waited until taping started, then brought a contract for my signature. I refused to sign it right then, primarily because I didn't see any reason for it at that point. I had paid everybody because I don't like to have bills hanging over me.

What a night!

Once I read it, I realized that if I had signed that contract, she would have owned Singsation.

My idea was to mix the quartets and choirs, but my producer kept taping the choirs and no quartets. I asked why. There may have been a technical reason for it, but nobody explained anything to me. She just blew me off. That's when the trouble started. She walked off and took all her people with her. I was left alone in the studio with the engineer. He had the grace to remind me that since I was the one footing the bill, I had the right to keep on using the facility. So I put on the headset and became the producer. I didn't know what I was doing, but I knew what I wanted, and I muddled through the rest of the taping. It became clear that she had her own agenda when I discovered she planned on using my material for her own project, a choir sing-off. It also became all too clear that she had made some heavy financial commitments that I had to meet. I had to use $400,000 that wiped out all my savings and $200,000 in loans to pay for everything. The next step, in my mind, was to get on the air so that I could make my money back.

I made the rounds of the local TV stations. ABC, NBC and Fox turned me down, but I had better luck at CBS. Jonathan Rodgers, the General Manager, gave me a shot and I was ready to go. We went on the air on June 4, 1989. What I didn't have was enough advertising revenue to offset my expenditures. My production costs averaged around $25,000 per show and I didn't have much revenue coming in. In short, I lost over $600,000 and Singsation almost died at birth.

This was a major test of faith. I had stepped out into space without a safety net, and I had to put my trust in the Lord that things would work out. I was in serious debt and had a lot to lose, but I was determined to make it work. The only solution was to get enough advertising to make it profitable, but a local show doesn't generate that kind of revenue. If you spend the kind of production money I was averaging, you will stay in the red forever. The answer was syndication.

Syndication is the process of getting stations in different cities to run your show. The more stations you get, the more money you can charge for the advertising. I didn't know anything about syndication when I started out, but once I got an understanding of how it worked, I got busy. I traveled to major cities myself and talked to the station managers personally. I tried to concentrate on cities that have a high concentration of gospel-loving people. Slowly but surely, I built up the number of stations that were airing Singsation and, in less than two years, I got out of the red and made back my initial investment.

I lucked out with my next producer. Hoyett Owens knew his way around the media, praise the Lord, and he and I saw eye to eye on how things should be done. More important, he was- and is- a Christian. Hoyett was very familiar with radio because he had been involved with a local radio station in Chicago, and we learned television production together.

Producer, Hoyett Owens, and guest artist, Vickie Winans and me.

In the beginning, Hoyett screened all the audition tapes, the way conscientious producers do, and he would put some tapes in the round file. When I found that out, I put a stop to it. I see the show as a vehicle for worship and, as hard as it was for me to become accepted as a singer, I'm not about to exclude anybody who wants to praise the Lord through song. If they want to sing unto the Lord, I want to let them. So our philosophy is to let anybody who wants to sing come on the show if we have room for them. It's come to a point that we are overbooked the minute people find out that we're going into production. It's only a half-hour show and we don't have room for everybody. That's unfortunate, but it is an indication of our continued success.

I can't think of any prominent gospel singer who hasn't appeared on the show at some time or the other. This is good news and bad news. When we were new kids on the block, the big name singers and groups tried to run it. Since our time was a precious half hour, we would ask performers to limit their numbers to five minutes or less. Well, you know how it is with Gospel music. A song can go on forever, if you let it. Some performers weren't ready to accept a limitation, and we had to learn to say a firm "no" to folks who wanted to have everything their way. I learned from association with them that Gospel singers can be as arrogant, pigheaded and spoiled as any other entertainers. Just like I learned that churchgoers can be some of the meanest people in the world.

Once Singsation caught on, I had an idea for a national choir competition. I took the idea to Quaker Oats and Voices of Tomorrow was born. We would hold the competition in several cities and tape the choirs so we could air them on the show. The winners received a sizeable donation for their churches, and the competition was the source of a lot of scholarship money.

I have a new producer because Hoyett has moved on to other things, but he is still an active member of the Singsation family. I consider him a friend and I'm grateful for all that he contributed to the success of the show. For one thing, he restored my faith in producers.

**Praise the Lord with harp: sing unto Him with the psaltery
and an instrument of ten strings.**
Psalms 33:2

When I had the idea for the show, one of my thoughts was that this was a way for the sick and shut-in to be part of a worship service. When I'm not singing on the show I'm sharing my faith in the Lord, and people listen. I get letters from my viewers all the time, telling me how much they enjoy the show and how it's been an inspiration. I'm particularly touched by letters from men in jail. Occasionally, they tell me that they have decided to accept Christ as their Savior, like the one that tracked me down at a concert soon after his release. He wanted to be baptized as soon as possible. That kind of thing makes Singsation very rewarding.

I was inspired to do the show because I wanted to render something to the Lord above and beyond tithes. I think He is pleased, because He blesses the show. Take for instance, the year protesters tried to shut down our concert in Philadelphia. He didn't let it happen. Since people knew I was connected to McDonald's, they chose to make our concert the center of an anti-McDonald's protest. They found some ministers to spearhead the protest against so-called slave wages. People were supposed to boycott, but they came anyway. And then it rained so hard on the picketers that they had to put down their signs and go home.

I get so much enjoyment and personal fulfillment from this show. When we tape in the studio, there is a mood and a spirit that brings all the choirs, the soloists, the quartets and the musicians together. Singsation is a true labor of love for all of us.

**Now faith is the substance of things hoped for,
the evidence of things not seen.**
Hebrews 11:1

My mama raised me to be a God-fearing, church-going young man, and that's what I was until the day I left Gilbert, Louisiana. Then I got lost. I believed in God, but I didn't believe in going to church. I went to the racetrack and night clubs, instead. Without Christ filling up my life, I had too much space for temptation. In my teens, I wasted my free time playing basketball, playing cards and playing the field. I didn't smoke and I never got into any really bad stuff like drugs or alcohol, but I was your typical hard-headed teen-aged boy who thinks he's a man. In my twenties, I spent my free time in night clubs, gambling and chasing women. When I got my stores, I played the horses, I tried to bankrupt Las Vegas and, yes, I loved the ladies. Life would always let me coast along for a while, then it would hit me with tough times.

In the early 70's, I got down on my luck, and I went into a depression so deep that my mama heard it echo in my voice one night when I called her. She told me I needed to get back in church. So I joined Christ Temple Missionary Baptist Church in 1973. Incidentally, I'm still a member there. I haven't changed my church because every church has its problems. So you might as well stay where you are and try to work them out. You don't gain anything by church hopping.

Anyway, I started going to church on a regular basis. I had a relationship with God, but no real commitment. I was a church member in good standing. I went to Bible study and prayer meetings, and I tithed. I was with the Norfleet Brothers, rehearsing and singing. But I was just paying lip service to the Lord, like so many of us do. On a scale of one to ten, with ten being the highest, I guess my commitment was around a four. Whenever the Lord bailed me out of a jam, my commitment would climb up the scale to as high as eight, but then it would start slipping as soon as life eased up on me. Like a child, I had a short attention span and when things were going good, I sort of forgot where all that good comes from.

On Sunday, I would sincerely have God on my mind, but during the week, my head would fill up with a lot of other things: my spouse, my job, my responsibilities, worries about my folks. My mind only went to Christ when I needed him to fix those things and ease those worries. If you find yourself thinking about your father, your mother, your children or your loved ones more than you think about Christ, there is something wrong with that scenario. When the reverse becomes true, and you focus on Christ, all those worries about other things will go away. Sadly, this wisdom doesn't come overnight.

My bout with prostate cancer tested my faith more than any other trial or tribulation, because lost loves can always be found somewhere, and money can be earned again, but dead is dead. Through that battle, I learned my most important lesson: I can put my total trust in Jesus Christ.

Part V
Walking A
New ROAD

Remember the Lord your God,
for it is He that giveth thee the power to get wealth.
Deuteronomy 8:18

In 1998, I had five McDonald's restaurants. All of them were in the Chicago area. They were busy, successful and very profitable. My TV show was a success, too. So was my new marriage. I had a nice home in Country Club Hills. My car was top of the line. I dressed well. I traveled first class, wherever and whenever the mood struck. Moreover, I had finally accomplished my primary goal. My parents were out of slavery. I had brought them to Chicago, and they lived in a nice town house. Contrary to all the odds, I had made it. Even so, I was not content.

I had been in the McDonald's system for 25 years, and it consumed a lot of my time. I wanted to be free to serve Christ, but I couldn't do that with a business that kept me busy 24/7.

One day, I walked into my store and looked around. Right then and there, I knew that this part of my life was over. I turned around, walked out, got into my car and drove around asking myself, "What shall I do next?" It was a big decision. I took my time. After talking to my friends in executive management, I decided that I would become a supplier. That's not a bad deal. McDonald's is huge and its suppliers can do very well. I examined my options and settled on disposable gloves, can liners and stuff like that, things that are necessary and constantly replaced.

Phasing out of the restaurant business into my new enterprise was a slow process. I wish that I could say that it was also easy. It wasn't. The other operators had a problem with what they called my "conflict of interest," but Jack Greenberg and Jim Skinner, two highly placed executives, stuck by me and I had the support of Mike Thompson, the head of the supply chain. My competitors didn't want me to get into the market, and I didn't speak Chinese. That was a problem because most disposable gloves are imported from Taiwan and mainland

China.

Fortunately, McDonald's was my biggest customer, and they have a history of fully supporting entrepreneurs. They introduced me to Dan Musachia and Mike Hickey of Perseco (now Havi Global Systems) their supply chain management company. That hook-up was the critical factor in the success of my transition to supplier. Dan is the president and CEO of this global organization, and he guided me through the complexities of all the supply procedures. I had no idea what I was getting into when I started out, and there was plenty of opportunity for me to stumble and fall, but Dan supported me all the way. He made sure that we had lunch on a regular basis so that he could keep me up to speed. I like to think that our conversations were two-way streets, because I could give him the owner-operator perspective on the supply-chain process, but in reality I was the primary beneficiary of the relationship.

Dan also paved my way by making sure we got paid on time, which is a crucial thing for entrepreneurs. Believe me, debt and the payment gap is what kills a lot of businesses in their infancy. Thanks to McDonald's and Perseco, we had a positive cash flow from day one. That allowed us to build a good relationship with the Chinese manufacturers. So now, we have a reputation for paying on time, which makes us a priority customer.

In 2003, I sold my last store and I was in the import business 100%. There were some anxious moments — hostile white competitors, reluctant Chinese wholesalers and skeptical new customers, but we survived. We could not afford to fail because too many churches were depending on our bottom line.

Today, Omar Medical Supplies, Inc. is a thriving enterprise with global connections. Through this business, I have been able to increase the number of churches I can help and the amount of my contributions.

Better is a dinner of herbs where love is,
than a stalled ox and hatred therewith.
Proverbs 15:17

Mike Hickey, the Vice President of Perseco, was the global connection that helped me get Omar, Inc., up and running as in import business. He took me overseas, introduced me to the supply sources and walked me through the confusing maze of Asian business practices. We spent enough time outside of offices and warehouses for me to develop a healthy respect for him that has grown into a friendship. We discovered that we both liked to go sightseeing when we visit new places.

On one of our trips, I encountered the kind of racism that I thought I had left behind in Gilbert. We were in Munich, and our hotel was located near Hitler's old headquarters. I think his ghost still walked the lobby, because when we checked in, I didn't exist. African Americans can relate to that sixth sense that we've developed- we can sense racism. It lifts the hairs on the back of your neck. I felt it in that lobby, and I was right. Both reservations were in my name, but the clerk reached around me to give the room key to Mike, the white man. When forced to deal with me, she said my room wasn't ready. I didn't think much of it, because that happens. So we went out to see what Munich looked like. When we returned, they showed me to this airless closet with a couch for a bed. Strike one.

When we went to a nearby restaurant for dinner, the waitress refused to take my order. So Mike called the manager over. He took my order, but by this time, I was scared to eat the food. I gave it to Mike. Strike two.

Germany will not get a strike three. If I ever have to do business over there, I will make it a day trip and fly somewhere else to spend the night. And I certainly don't plan to travel there for pleasure. I don't like spending money to feel bad.

**Behold, how good and
how pleasant it is for brethren**
Psalms 133:1

When I left home to seek my fortune, my mama gave me some advice that I have since learned is very, very sound. She said, "Judge people by the way they treat you." Coming from the racist environment I was raised in, it wasn't easy, but I have learned to deal with white people without distrusting them at first sight. Even so, I am still often uncomfortable when I meet white people for the first time. I admit it, I'm conditioned to expect the worst, but I have also learned that evil does not have a specific skin color, neither does good.

Working for McDonald's went a long way toward bringing me to the point of tolerance and understanding that my faith demands. Through my association with the Golden Arches, I have worked with good men, and bad, of both colors, but I have to say that the good far outnumber the bad. First and foremost, was Ray Kroc. I truly believe that he was color blind, and I don't think Dan Musachia and Mike Hickey have a prejudiced bone in their bodies. The same holds true for two men in the highest ranks of the McDonald's Corporation, Jack Greenberg and "the late Jim Cantalupo."

When I decided to sell my stores, Jim didn't want me to leave the system because he thought I had a valuable perspective on the business. If there were problems in the system, we would discuss them across the lunch table. We didn't always see eye to eye, but there was an honest dialogue. We had a good solid business relationship. It grew into such a close friendship that I literally cried when I heard that he had passed away.

The past president, Mike Roberts, would get into the bunker with you and do battle, and the current President, Don Thompson, makes an effort to embrace minority vendors. This is especially impressive to me because Don is an African American, and all too often we are guilty of what I call the "gatekeeper syndrome." As soon as some of us make it through the door of corporate America, we try to close it on everybody else that looks like us. Don is a notable exception to this rule because he tries to ensure that the system embraces diversity. I applaud him because it's not always a popular position to take, and it is not easy for an African American in corporate America to swim upstream.

I'm happy to say that Don is not the only committed African American executive that I know. Clarence Otis, the CEO of Darden Restaurants, gave Omar, Inc., a significant piece of business after we opened, but that is not why I applaud him. Yes, he supports diversity, but after we mentioned our Katrina efforts, he pitched in, too. He didn't say anything, he just started writing big checks for the relief effort.

Lee Dunham is another atypical example. Lee is a McDonalds's owner on the east coast, and he has a multitude of stores. He is also a charter member of the NBMOA. When the other members resisted my becoming an owner, Lee stood by me. He is a very strong, very vocal supporter for the Association and black suppliers.

So color doesn't have to make a difference. That's something us sensitive black people have to learn. In business, the dominant color is green. I know white people can say some things that make us cringe, or ball up our fists, but they aren't always coming from a racist perspective. Like they say in the Godfather movies, "It's not personal, it's business." We have to face some brutal realities if we want to seriously compete. We may think that we are being blocked out because we are black, but the reality may be that it's simply because we can't afford the entry fee. A lot of us just don't understand how much money it takes to make money. For instance, I didn't know about all the expensive liability insurance you need to carry in order to do business with most corporations. To some black people it might seem like one more thing to keep us out of the party, but it's not an artificial barrier, it's a requirement no matter what color you are. On the other hand, white corporate America doesn't understand that we don't have access to resources that white America takes for granted. So when African Americans have an opportunity and fall short, they may get a bad rap for the wrong reasons.

The bottom line is that white people have to be more sensitive to what black people have been through, and black people have to stop, listen and think before jumping to conclusions. I'm not so naïve that I dismiss racism. It exists, but we can overcome it if we can learn to look past racial differences and consider the individual. We must learn to judge people, as Dr. King said, "by the content of their character."

Train up a child in the way he should go:
and when he is old, he will not depart from it.
Proverbs 22:6

They say that success comes at a price. I guess I paid for my success in lost relationships with my first wife and my children, particularly my children. I was not there for my kids because I was always too busy. I didn't see anything wrong with that back then because my father was rarely around me, and I didn't turn out so bad. Still, some of my kids have disappointed me in ways that I never disappointed my father, and I'll never be sure how much of it was my fault.

After my divorce, my ex drove a wedge between me and the kids and I know that they suffered from the lack of a father's presence in their lives, particularly the boys. At some point, all of them worked in my stores, but their mother put a stop to that. She led them to believe that they should have a free ride because I was financially able to provide it. I didn't agree with that at all, and I think that's the problem today between me and my daughter, Kenya. I don't have any kind of contact with her.

My son Omar

Omar, Terrell and Rashod drifted into a gang lifestyle and started dealing with drugs. One thing is for sure, if you deal with drugs you go to jail or you go to your grave. Omar did both. When he went to jail, I wanted him to serve his time because I really believed that if he got out, he would be dead within a year, but he called me one day, crying. He told me he couldn't take it and he begged me to get him out. So I did, against my better judgment. Eight months later, he was dead at age 20. A gangbanger followed him home, shot him dead and came close to killing his sister, Kenya. Omar's death was a tragedy, but it made my other boys realize that that was not the kind of end that they wanted.

For a while, Terrell was a contract truck driver, with a very

My son, Terrell

healthy income, but he never had any money. So he came to me for financial advice. He was in debt and owed a lot of back taxes. I reluctantly bailed him out so that he could have a fresh start.

He's an important part of Omar, Inc., now. He has a head for the business and he knows the streets. So I'm grooming him to take over the company once the Lord retires me. My challenge is getting him to leave emotions out of the business and not make some of the mistakes I made by letting personal relationships interfere with business decisions. If you make a mistake when you're working for somebody else, that's one thing, but when you're the CEO, your mistakes put all your employees at risk. You don't have to be ruthless or heartless with people, but you don't need to be brainless, either.

Rashod stopped working for me some time ago, and he is off doing his own thing. So I don't see him anywhere near as often as I see Terrell, but we are not strangers.

My other daughter, my first baby, was born when I was sixteen, but I didn't become a father to her until she was about that same age. Her mother didn't press me into marriage, which is a good thing. I had a man's body and a man's urges, but I wasn't a man, yet. I was young and broke, and I didn't think I could take care of a child, so I didn't. I felt bad about it, but my mind wasn't in it and I neglected her. I admit that.

I wasn't involved in this daughter's life at all until she got into high school. By then, I had my McDonald's franchise and I was much better off, financially. One day she walked into my store and I jumped at the chance to try to make up for past neglect and finally act like a father.

Since she wanted to go to college, I made a covenant with her that if she kept up her grades and worked in my store during the summer, I would pay her way through college. This worked out well her Freshman and Sophomore years. I bought her a car and she had a summer job in my store. Then it fell apart.

At the end of her second year, she told me she wasn't going back to school and that she didn't want to work for me that summer. Instead, she was going away with her boyfriend. So much for our arrangement. I don't think she realized how serious I was about her keeping up her end of the bargain. I didn't hear from her any more until it was time for her to go back to school and I refused to pay her tuition.

I didn't think any more about it until the man from the sheriff's office knocked on my door. He reluctantly showed me a subpoena with my name on it and told me he didn't want to give it to me because he knew me by reputation. That didn't matter. Even if he didn't give it to me somebody else would have, eventually. So I took it. That's when I found out that my daughter was taking me to court in, of all places, Peoria, Illinois. So my attorney and I had to drive down there to face a judge and explain why I was neglecting my daughter again.

After I explained the terms of our agreement, it was her turn to explain why she didn't come back to work at the store that summer. This is where it got ugly. My daughter told the judge that she wasn't comfortable working for me because I had made sexual advances to her when we went to my grandmother's funeral down in Gilbert.

I had sworn on a Bible, so you know that what I told the judge was the truth. Yes, we flew down to Gilbert for my grandmother's funeral. Yes, we stayed at my parent's house overnight. Mama only had one extra bedroom which she gave to me. She made a pallet on the floor in the living room for my daughter, but she didn't want to sleep there. She came to my room and asked if she could share my bed. My sane mind whispered, "Wilson, this is not a good idea." I didn't listen .

After my testimony, the judge called for a recess and set another court date because he wanted my mother to testify. You cannot imagine how angry I was about that. I did not want to drag Mama into this mess, but I had to. My mother testified in my favor, of course. Then my lawyer cross-examined my daughter and caught her in a lie. She couldn't untangle herself, so she broke down and started crying. "I'm so sorry. I'm so sorry." She confessed that nothing had happened and she told the judge the whole thing had been her mother's idea.

I was through with her at that point. This court case had cost me close to $75,000 in attorneys fees, travel expenses and the time away from my business. That I could forgive. What I couldn't get over was what she accused me of doing. I didn't think anybody could stoop that low, and I don't care whose idea it was.

For a while, she continued to call me and my mother, to apologize. She followed me around and she would show up at churches where I was speaking or singing. She finally stopped, and that chapter is closed.

I sometimes wonder if I could have done things differently, and would my kids have turned out differently. Then I look around and I see husbands and wives who stay together and still can't do anything with their kids. So there is no guarantee that my kids would have turned out any better.

I do love my children. They are in my heart, even if they are not in my life. All my businesses have been named after them. When I had my McDonald's stores, they were all DBA's: doing business as Kenya, Omar, Terrell and Rashod. When I went into medical supplies, I transferred the name of my deceased son to my new business. My children always have the option to be a part of my life, if they come the right way. They will always be my children and I will always help them, within reason. In the meantime, I have a growing family in Christ. I have the many mothers, fathers, wives, brothers, sisters, sons and daughters that I have gained through my ministry.

Honor thy father and thy mother: that thy days may be long upon the land which the Lord thy God giveth thee.
Exodus 20:12

My blood family is not what you'd call close. Some of my sisters were born after I left home, and my brothers and I were all spread out. The most time I spent with my father was when I was finally able to bring my parents up from Louisiana. At first, our roles were reversed. I was the one who was always busy working. That was okay for the first five years, but then Daddy got sick. "Please, God," I prayed, "I just got him out of slavery. If you take him now, I won't have any time to be with him." I asked Christ to please give me some time with him and my prayers were answered. The Lord gave him another decade. I took advantage of those extra years and we did things together and made up for the times that we missed when I was a child. I really appreciated those extra years.

We buried him down in Wisner, because that's where he wanted to be. I think his desire was for Mama to be down there, too, but she hasn't told me what her wishes are. I even thought about buying a family plot but I got voted down by the rest of the family. "Don't you be buying me a plot! Buy your own self a plot!" I didn't realize what a sensitive issue it was.

After Daddy passed, I thought Mama would move in with me, but she wasn't having any of that. Despite two hip replacements, she's determined to be independent. She lives in her own townhouse and runs it her way.

Mom and Dad at the opening of one
of my stores. These were good days.

Am I my brother's keeper?
Genesis 4:9

My sister, Dale, works with me and I see her just about every day, but I don't have much to do with my other brothers and sisters. We don't visit each other and we never pick up the phone just to talk. It used to be that we'd meet down in Gilbert with my parents, but once I brought Mama and Daddy up to Chicago those little reunions stopped. I guess it's because we didn't grow up as a close family. Even though Dale has become my right arm at the company, I really don't know much about her. She was only about three or four years old when I left home. Some of my other sisters weren't even born.

Dale Wilson

When Dale left Gilbert, she moved to Los Angeles, got married and had a daughter. Although I knew where she was, we didn't have much contact. Then one night I was stranded in LA, never mind how or why, and I needed a ride. I called Dale. She picked me up and we established a loose link. When her marriage went sour, she moved to Chicago and started working for me at one of my stores. It was only for a hot minute the first time, and not much longer the second time, because we had communication problems. For one thing, I was a workaholic and, like most people, Dale was not. My sisters had it easier than my brothers and I did, because my parents changed the rules after we left home. They thought maybe they had been too strict with us boys. Mama says she thinks all that whippin' ran us away from home. So they eased up on the girls. Dale is very smart and by the time she finished high school, things down home had improved so much, financially, that she was even able to go to college.

The third time Dale came to work for me was a charm. She's been with me now for two decades. She's my Co-CEO at Omar, Inc. We've been working together long enough now that she knows my mind and can make decisions without my input. Although she always checks with me, I have learned to trust her judgment. I must say "Talk to Dale about that" at least a dozen times a day, and I have no problem sending her out to my clients to represent me. I trust her with my business and I trust her with my money. That says it all.

**For He will give his angels charge of you
to guard you in all your ways.**
Psalms 91:11

I have to laugh when I hear the term "self-made millionaire," because nobody makes it totally on his own. There is always someone along the way to help make it happen. In my case there are several "someones" that I hold in my heart with thanks: Ray Kroc, the angel who helped me get my first franchise when I didn't have a dime; Reggie Webb, who helped me gain my footing as a franchisee; Johnathan Rodgers, who gave me the opportunity to make Singsation a reality; and Rosie.

Rosie Daniels

When Rosie Daniels walked into my store looking for a job, I hired her because she told me she was from Alabama. That was all the resume that I needed. To me, being from the South meant she was no stranger to hard work. I felt that a woman from down home would be dedicated, dependable and loyal. I was right. Rosie has high principles and unshakeable values. She is one of those people who will give you 110 percent on a bad day and, believe me, it's good to have somebody like that watching your back when you have a fast food kind of operation.

Rosie worked in my stores until she could run one as well as I could, and when I went through a bad time that's exactly what she did. One winter I had a tooth pulled and I caught cold in my jaw. The side of my face ballooned up, and I caught a virus I couldn't shake. I was a mess. I finally decided to go somewhere hot so that I could get over everything. I left Rosie in charge. She took care of everything and wouldn't let me come back until I was 100%.

When I decided to leave the McDonald's system, I helped Rosie get her own store. Then she got sick. I didn't realize how sick until I saw her. She had dropped so much weight I didn't recognize her. It scared me to death. We had a long talk and she agreed that the store was too much. So she sold her store and came to work for me at Omar, Inc., doing whatever needs to be done, and whatever she wants to do. She doesn't really have to work, but it would probably drive her crazy to stay at home doing nothing. As long as she wants to be a part of Omar, Inc., she has a place because she's more than a sister to me. She's another one of my angels.

Judge not according to the appearance
John7:24

Being active in the community means that you sometimes get involved in controversy, and one of the most controversial events of the 90's was the Million Man March. It was the brainchild of one of the decade's most controversial figures, Louis Farrakhan. This is one man who evokes strong opinions. People either love him, hate him, fear him or venerate him.

Louis Farrakhan is alright with me. In the first place, anybody who tries to help black people rise above poverty, ignorance, self-hate and self-destruction is alright with me. In the second place, Minister Farrakhan had my back when gangbangers threatened my life.

I became acquainted with Farrakhan when the NBMOA had a convention in Chicago. We went to the Minister's house and I struck up a conversation with him. I told him that I liked what he was doing in terms of battling drugs and gangs. I wrote him a check for $5,000 right, then and there. We got to be good friends, even though I told him I wasn't going to change my religion.

One day at lunch, he mentioned his idea for a Million Man March. I wanted to know the purpose. He said, "Regaining pride, voter registration, community activism," and other stuff like that. "Well," I told him, "I'm a business man. What about the economic piece?" That was my primary focus and, eventually, Farrakhan left that part up to me and that became my role. I started working closely with Ben Chavis and the NAACP. It was always a mystery to me that Dr. Chavis could fly from one city to another and rarely had cab fare from the airport. Many times I had to pick him up. Anyway, when we firmed up plans for the march, the organizers asked me to speak about business and to supervise the financial end, specifically any money that was collected.

There was a lot of resistance to the idea of the march. White folks were afraid of Louis Farrakhan and black ministers were suspicious of him. So churches were hesitant to support what should have been a massive ground swell of black cooperation. They were dealing with the man, not the principles of the march. The white press hinted that it was racist and black women thought it was sexist. Even so, despite the resistance the overall reaction was positive and the turnout was more than the press could accept. We knew pretty early on that it would probably be more than one million, regardless of what the media said. You could feel the spirit in the air. They were even talking about it in South Africa when I went over there in early October. They even tried to bump me from my flight home so that some highly-placed people could get to Washington for the event, but I would not be moved. I had a purpose and a responsibility. I was going to address the crowd, and Minister Farrakhan had asked me to be charge of any money collected.

I made my speech, but when the collection was over, the money drove off and I was left behind. I finally caught up with the collectors at a counting area. Money was everywhere, with dozens of counters who stood at attention when I came in. Everybody was showing toothy smiles as they brought me a card so that I could sign off on the total. I wasn't inclined to do that. Not when they brought me in after the fact. If every body at that march had only put in a dollar, the total had to be way more than the figure that they showed me. I don't know what happened to the rest. So I refused to approve the total. That was the end of my association with the March, but not with the minister.

When Omar was killed, I received death threats from gang bangers. They even threatened to disrupt the services and turn over his casket. Minister Farrakhan sent a contingent of Muslim brothers as a security force. I felt like the President of the United States. When I went up to speak, they were four deep around the altar. There was no way anyone could have approached me. They protected me and my family at the cemetery, as well. I really appreciated that. I may not agree with everything that Louis Farrakhan says and everything that he does, but I cannot and will not deny him. I condemn hatred because the Bible preaches love. So I have to disassociate myself from the words, but not the man.

I continue unto this day, witnessing both to small and great.
Acts 26:22

I never got past the seventh grade and I didn't go to college. Down in the land of cane and cotton, I was lucky to get three months of schooling a year, learning the rudiments of readin', writin' and 'rithmetic. The rest of the time, I was in the fields. One year, I missed school altogether, but I didn't feel that I missed much. I have gained the essential knowledge I've needed through life experience, and my lack of a diploma has never hindered me. In fact, I have five honorary doctorate degrees in recognition of my philanthropy and my furtherance of Gospel music: Doctor of Divinity from Mt. Carmel Theological Seminary; a Doctors of

Dr. Willie Wilson

Humane Letters from Chicago Baptist Institute; Doctor of Humanitarianism from both Swisher Bible College and the Denver Institute of Urban Studies and Adult College; and a Doctor of Music and Art from Midwest Theological Institute.

I take my Doctorate of Divinity very seriously, but I don't use it to impress. I use it to express my faith in Jesus Christ through the motivational speaking that is part of my ministry. It helps me render unto the Lord. Almost every Sunday of the year, you will find me- Dr. Wilson- in the pulpit of a different church. I am invited to speak in the morning and, because of the popularity of Singsation, to give a well-attended free concert in the afternoon. When I'm in the pulpit, I don't preach. I just tell my story because it's such a powerful testament to God's goodness. Before I leave, my wife presents a check to the Pastor, usually for $5,000.

I've been doing this for twenty years, and I concentrate on small churches that need financial assistance. I used to give to Operation Push, NAACP and the other popular organizations people give to on a regular basis, but I stopped so I could focus on the many small churches that struggle to pay their bills. There is always need in a small flock — sickness, bereavement, families in financial distress. My contributions help ease the burden.

When I started out, I would call churches and ask them to let me come and sing, and I would give them money to let me do it. Actually, I gave the money because I knew these churches needed it. Word gets around and nowadays the churches call me. The demand is so great that I can't always get to all the individual churches anymore. So now I sometimes go someplace like Macomb, Mississippi, and meet with a group of ministers at one time. In cases like this, I leave a five-figure check for the group. Giving is a wonderful feeling. I feel good knowing that I have helped and that I'm doing my part to build the kingdom. I'm happier doing this than I've ever been in my life. I never get tired of doing good. I never get tired. Even when I'm physically tired, I feel exhilarated.

Whatever I do in business is to support this ministry. It is gratifying, satisfying and it keeps me out of trouble. It fills the empty spaces within me and, as long as I keep my mind on Christ and surround myself with spirituality in my schedule, I can't mess around and do the wrong thing. Since the Bible says it is hard for a rich man to enter into the kingdom of God, I don't want to do anything that will jeopardize my chance of going to heaven.

Speak ye every man the truth to his neighbor.
Zechariah 8:16

Since I was in charge of the economic arm of the Million Man March, I traveled around promoting the event. Dorothy J. Gaiter was in the audience when I was speaking to a group of businessmen at the Westin Hotel in Miami. She introduced herself as a staff reporter for a major newspaper in New York, and she said that she wanted to do a story about me. At first I didn't want to do it because the white media had been very negative about Minister Farrakhan, and I was afraid that it would turn out to be another Farrakhan bashing— with me in the middle. As a McDonald's operator I was concerned that it would reflect badly on the corporation. So I said, "No." She was persistent and kept after me. I needed assurance that an African-American reporter could guarantee that an objective story would come out of that white environment. Since she came across as honest and sincere, she finally convinced me that her article would be about me and not a negative focus on Minister Farrakhan. That's how I wound up on the front page of the The Wall Street Journal on October 16, 1996, a year after the March.

Miss Gaiter did a nice job of telling my story, and I know it reached a lot of people because I got congratulatory calls from friends, colleagues and complete strangers. One of those strangers was a very prominent, very successful Hollywood producer/director. He wanted to make my life story into a movie. Of course, I was flattered and we had a few conversations. Then the thing broke down. In true Hollywood fashion, they wanted to add some stuff that I didn't agree with, like me taking drugs. I guess Hollywood didn't think my life was exciting enough. I couldn't go that way, so the deal fell through.

All of this happened before the Holy Spirit guided me to China, and before I met some Hollywood people who understand my point of view. So who knows? You might still see my story up on the big screen someday.

Reprinted from THE WALL STREET JOURNAL.

TUESDAY, OCTOBER 15, 1996   © *1996 Dow Jones & Company, Inc. All Rights Reserved.*

American Journey

How Willie L. Wilson Went From Poverty To Black Philanthropy

He Swept Floors at First And Later Mopped Up In the Gospel Business

Of Farrakhan and Angels

By Dorothy J. Gaiter
Staff Reporter of The Wall Street Journal

CHICAGO — Long ago, Willie L. Wilson ran off from a Florida work camp, convinced it was virtual slavery. Hounds chased him, but he got away.

Later, though he had no money, and only an eighth-grade education, he convinced himself he could run his own business. No matter that his career began as a floor-mopper in a fast-food restaurant. Like his belief in God, there are some things he just knows to be true.

Still later, though Mr. Wilson could barely carry a note, he desperately wanted a place in the church choir. He doesn't sing much better these days, but has made a fortune turning his love of gospel music into a multimillion-dollar business.

The 48-year-old Mr. Wilson is a rare bird on the American landscape — a self-made black millionaire and philanthropist. Neither a sports hero nor a celebrity, he has made his money the old-fashioned way, as a quintessential can-do American in an America that hasn't always been kind to his aspirations.

Yet hurdles — lack of education, racism and more than his share of personal turmoil and tragedy — have only made him want to jump higher. "As a black male, I'm not supposed to be here," Mr. Wilson says. "I'm supposed to be in jail or on drugs. The system didn't expect anything to become of me."

Independent Thinker

Quiet, unassuming, a little rough at the edges, Mr. Wilson these days lives in a system of his own making, preaching a kind of black self-sufficiency while giving away—with no regard to ideology— annual six-figure sums to African-American causes. Though hardly a household name in even the black community, he has recently chaired economic-development committees of the NAACP, Jesse Jackson's Operation PUSH and Louis Farrakhan's and Benjamin Chavis's National African American Leadership Summit.

Underlying his generosity is a real toughness: "If you're not Jesus, I'm not afraid of you," he says. Thus, pondering whether giving to someone as controversial as Mr. Farrakhan is the right thing to do, he says, "I may not agree with everything they say and do, but if their heart is in trying to help black people, then I'm going to give them help."

Those who know Mr. Wilson are hardly surprised by his success, or his generosity. "He has a Ph.D. from the university of the street — what old folks would call 'Mother Wit,'" says Reginald Webb, a Pomona, Calif., business associate. Adds Jimmie L. Daniels, a former president of Operation PUSH, which has benefited from Mr. Wilson's giving: "Willie is straightforward" and dedicated to the notion that African-Americans will benefit more from "jobs than government entitlements."

That Mr. Wilson can't easily be pigeonholed reflects a life that itself is full of complexities, ironies and luck — good and bad. His story, corroborated by friends, business associates and family members, features a failed marriage, the death of a son to gang violence and an embrace of black-nationalist politics that leave him critical of African-American organizations that depend on white charity for their existence. His story also features two guardian angels—one black, one a wealthy white man: the late Ray Kroc, the founder of McDonald's Corp.

Life for Mr. Wilson began with few outward prospects. He was born in Gilbert, La., one of 11 children of sharecroppers Douglas and Lula Mae Wilson. As a child, he chopped cotton and hay for 25 cents a day. School was a luxury in-between the long crop seasons.

At 13, he left home to find a job and landed in a work camp in South Florida, where the pay for picking vegetables never quite seemed to equal the cost of room and board charged by the camp's owners. So one night, with dogs at their heels, Mr. Wilson and several young men fled. Along the way, a man appeared and told them of a safe place to find work. A few yards down the road, Mr. Wilson says, he remembered that they hadn't thanked the stranger, but he was gone. "To this day," Mr. Wilson says, "I think he was an angel of God."

Hard Times

Mr. Wilson did find work, making $13 a day picking crops, and later he moved to Miami, where he washed dishes in a restaurant, all the while sending money home. After several months, he found himself seriously ill and had to ask his mother for money to return to Louisiana. "I hated to do it because she had to borrow money from the white man, and borrowing $15 was like borrowing $1,000," he says.

After convalescing, Mr. Wilson moved away again and began bouncing between Chicago and New York, for several years working at low-wage jobs, including assembling pianos, parking cars, installing ceiling tiles and changing tires.

By 1970, he found himself broke and collecting unemployment compensation. "I was in a rut," he says. His landlady suggested he apply for work at a new McDonald's nearby.

As unpromising as it sounded, the advice would change his life.

A Fateful Move

Mr. Wilson got a job mopping floors, cleaning garbage cans and cooking hamburgers for $2 an hour. He made a good first impression on the white owner. Soon after he was hired, the restaurant's managers walked out in a dispute with the owner; in desperation, he asked Mr. Wilson to run the place.

He did so well that, after the managers returned, the owner insisted that Mr. Wilson remain in management. But he balked at first, being unsure about managing a crew that was largely white. Still, he persevered, despite hostility from other managers who never forgave him for holding things together during their walkout. By quietly going over the receipts each night, he even managed to fill in his one managerial weakness — learning how to keep the books.

In time, Mr. Wilson found himself in another management role at a new McDonald's opened by the same owner. But the racial tension of his previous job turned to open hostility. Some whites he disciplined complained to their friends and parents, and Mr. Wilson endured threats — once he was told to leave town.

"I had planned to leave anyway," he recalls, "but I decided I wouldn't let them run me away." He stuck it out, won some of his adversaries over — then later was fired when he asked for a promotion.

Years had passed and Mr. Wilson had married in the interim. The 14-hour days at McDonald's had taken their toll and his marriage, he says, turned increasingly bitter. Two days after his firing, his wife

(over please)

Whom shall I send, and who will go for us?
Then said I, Here am I; send me.
Isaiah 6:8

My ministry is guided by the Holy Spirit, and I follow where it leads. When Hurricane Katrina started screaming her way across the Gulf Coast on August 26th, 2005, it lead me south. On August 29th, Katrina slammed into New Orleans, breached the levees in 58 different places and flooded about 80% of the city. Along with the rest of America, I watched TV coverage of the devastation with my wife, Janette. We were stunned by the horror of it: lives, businesses and futures, washed away in the rising waters. This was a terrible, terrible thing.

Now, usually, when there's a major natural disaster someplace, especially overseas, you help by writing a check to the Red Cross or some other relief agency. This felt different. This time, it was right here in the United States, within driving distance, in my home state. So I asked my wife, "Why should we wait for the Red Cross to do something that we can do ourselves?" I figured there was nothing to stop us from taking direct action.

I ignored my first inclination to do something in Louisiana, because it bothered me that all the attention was focused on New Orleans. The world has heard of the Big Easy, Beale Street, Louis Armstrong, and so on, and that's where they centered most of the news coverage. But

Katrina did some serious damage across the river, too. There were one or two brief mentions, but the effects in Mississippi were mostly overlooked. So that's where I wanted to focus my personal relief efforts. I wanted to go somewhere that the major relief efforts were not. After all, I figured that New Orleans would be well-taken care of. It wasn't until later that I found out how wrong I was about that.

The first thing I did was call as many ministers as I could, and I asked them for pledges of $1,000 apiece. Then we organized a concert with the Singsation band and choir. People turned out to support it, and we raised around $60,000. Next, I chartered a bus and, with the help of the mayor of Hazel Crest, we filled two trucks with clothes and blankets. Janette asked me if we could get another truck because the Holy Spirit put it on her mind to take some "things you men don't think about." She called all the ministers wives and the women of the churches filled the truck with things like deodorant, baby formula, underwear, feminine hygiene products and diapers. She was right, that kind of thing never crossed my mind. I didn't think about the fact that even with money, if the stores are gone, you can't buy basic stuff. She was right about the need, too. Once we got south, those trucks emptied out faster than a classroom on the last day of school.

We targeted two cities in Mississippi, Biloxi and Prentiss. My "rescue mission" included about forty ministers, their wives and the Singsation Band. Some of them were concerned about making motel reservations on the road, but I told them that we weren't going to sleep anywhere but on the bus. I planned for us to drive straight there, do what we had to do, and then drive straight back. When they grumbled, I reminded them that the people we were going to help had been going without sleep, hot water, soft beds and clean clothes. "We can't understand what they're going through unless we share some of their pain."

With that, we got on the bus and headed south. The mayor of Hazel Crest sent two policemen to go down there with us. One of them was the second in command of the police force. This was essentially a police escort that started growing before we crossed the southern Indiana border. I don't know if the mayor called ahead or if the policemen sent word. Whatever the case, more policemen joined us when we stopped to eat. By the time we reached Biloxi, we had a sizeable entourage.

And a multitude was waiting for us, camped out in and around an open stadium. You could see the despair and desperation in their faces. Black, white, yellow...all colors. When the white people noticed that my group was mostly black, they asked if they could get in line, too, or was it for black people only. I told them it was for human people. One lady broke down and cried when she heard my answer.

We started passing out money, and we gave $200 cash to every man, woman and child. Checks wouldn't have worked because nobody had any ID to cash them. It was a good feeling to know that we were contributing to their recovery in some way. So, despite our unwashed and sleepless state, we were in an uplifted mood as we left those hundreds of grateful people in Biloxi. We headed on down the road to Prentiss, about one hundred miles away.

The crowd that greeted us was bigger than the one in Biloxi, and when I reached the church auditorium, it was filled with people. The normal population of Prentiss is around 1,000. I think half of them were crowded in and around the auditorium. They almost stampeded me, but the police and my band gathered around to keep me from being overwhelmed. I thought that was all of them until I took a break to go to the washroom. A man approached me and asked me to step into the church and say a few words to the people who had been waiting inside. You can't imagine how I felt when I discovered the other half of the population waiting for me inside the church. "Lord, have mercy! I don't know if we have enough money to go round."

We thought that we had enough cash when we left Chicago, but something told me to bring more. So I put an extra $40,000 in my pocket that no one knew about. These were my personal funds that I brought as a contingency, to stretch the contributions. I wasn't sure that we would need it when we left home, but when I stepped inside that church, I wasn't even sure if that would be enough. So we reduced the stipend. Instead of $200, we started giving $100. Then we went down to $50. Eventually, we reduced it to $25 each. At one point, I had the ministers and my band empty their pockets and ante up, just in case we ran out of money. It was close but, fortunately, we were able to accommodate everybody. It touched my heart that they were so grateful for whatever we could give. One man said, "If I could just get a toothbrush." These people hadn't just lost their homes, they had lost all the simple things that we take for granted like toothpaste, soap, and underwear. Even $25 was a Godsend to them.

By the grace of God, the money stretched. I even had enough left over to give the pastor a $1,000 and reimburse everybody that went into their pockets. But I felt bad that I couldn't give everybody $200, like we did in Biloxi. I felt like I had shortchanged the people of Prentiss, so I promised that I would come back. I kept my promise on Christmas Day.

Ordinarily, my Christmas Day is quiet and uneventful. After church, it's a day for relaxation and doing a bunch of nothing. The Christmas after Katrina, the Spirit moved me to go back to Prentiss. My wife had just had minor surgery right before the holiday, and her mother was staying with us. So I knew she was in good hands. I flew down with about $80,000 in my pocket for the people of Prentiss. I went back to the church, and it was packed, again. This time, in addition to the money, I had an opportunity to address the massive congregation. I spoke from my heart and assured them that God does not make mistakes. Even though this had been a terrible tragedy, there was some good that came from it. Lives may have been lost, but souls were saved.

Yea, though I walk through the valley of the shadow of death,
I shall fear no evil; for thou art with me.
Psalm 23

I don't care how successful or rich you are, cancer is a wake-up call. When you hear the "C" word, the first thing you think is, "I'm gonna die." You start asking yourself, "Is this it? What can I do to make this go away?" In most tough situations, you can eventually find an out... get a loan, get a job, or get away. So far, there is no medicine that will cure cancer, but Christ can. I know this for a fact.

I got my wake-up call late in 2006. I went in for a routine check-up and my doctor told me that my PSA levels were up. I didn't know what they were. "What does that mean?" "It means you may have prostate cancer." I went into immediate denial and ignored it completely. Four months later, the level had gone up drastically. I waited another three months and it was up again. I finally had a biopsy. It was positive, but I wanted a second opinion; and a third; and a fourth. My doctor kept urging me to have surgery, but I kept dragging my feet. By the time I was ready to do something about it, my doctor was ready to go on vacation and told me I would have to wait. By then I understood the urgency. I had done some serious research and knew that time was crucial. At a certain point, there is no chance of survival. Had I waited too long?

I dropped to my knees. "Lord, I need to do this right away." Almost immediately, the phone rang. It was the hospital, asking if I could come in for the procedure. I was ready and I was resigned. "Lord, I'm not going to ask you to bring me out of this, but I have a lot of work left to do. Thy will be done." I had my surgery and I didn't need any further treatment —no radiation, no chemo. I am blessed and I am truly thankful.

Less than three weeks after my surgery, I had to tape my TV show. I was urged not to do it, but I trusted that the Lord would carry me through. Once I got into the spirit of the music, all my concerns disappeared and I felt like I could go all night. Fortunately, that wasn't necessary. The whole process was mentally and physically taxing, and my bandages had to be changed in the middle of the taping, but I made it through without any side effects.

Cancer has been my biggest test of my faith so far. It has taken me a lifetime to learn that with Christ, all things are possible. There is no doubt left in me now. Some things can be chalked up to chance or circumstance, but my cure was purely the goodness of Christ. Period.

With men this is impossible, but with God all things are possible.
Matthew 19:26

On April 4, 2008, I signed a contract that allowed me to become a foreigner doing business in the region of Inner Mongolia, China. I now own 25% of a glove factory over there. Although there was a formal ceremony and the Chinese treated it as a momentous occasion, you probably didn't read about it in any of our newspapers. People around the world were protesting China's treatment of Tibet, so nobody had anything good to say about the Peoples' Republic.

I'm sure that there will be critics who want to know why I would want a factory in China. "Why didn't you build a factory in the United States?" Well, the answer is two-fold. First of all, I get 100 per cent of my gloves from China, so this way I am right at the source. Now I won't be held hostage to price changes in the marketplace. I can be competitive by passing my economies along to my customers. This is common sense and it makes sound business sense. Secondly, it was a much simpler undertaking.

I plan to build or acquire a glove factory right here in the United States, too, but China was a bird in the hand. It was easier to accomplish this expansion overseas than over here in the United States, because Inner Mongolia was anxious for me to come over there. That region has a high level of unemployment, and there are no unions to paralyze businesses.

Now, before you imagine sweat shops, I want you to know that I pay a better than fair or decent wage. I'm not so far removed from making 20 cents an hour that I would ever exploit any human being. In fact, I pay my Chinese employees so well that my Chinese business associates resent me. "You spoil them. You make it difficult for us..."

and so on and so on. I don't think I'm spoiling anybody. I believe that a worker deserves a decent living wage, so that's what I pay. Once I get my factory over there, I plan to build a glove factory here and I will treat my American employees the same way. I will pay them a fair, better-than-average wage for honest work. That's the only way a Christian can do business.

Even as I write this book I am in the process of building a new warehouse about three miles from our current location and that's where I will build my glove factory. This will create jobs on this side of the Pacific. The trick will be keeping the overhead low enough to stay competitive. We're in a global economy and when I go on line to bid, the Chinese are online, too, underbidding everybody. Between my factory in China and my factory here in the U.S., I will strive to keep the playing field as level as possible.

The ultimate goal of all this expansion, whether it is in China, Africa or the United States, is the growth of Omar, Inc. My company exists, not to make me rich, but to fund my ministries. The more money that falls to the bottom line, the more money that is available to give to churches in need. It's not about global expansion, it's about Kingdom building.

**And we know that all things work together for good
to them that love God.**
Romans 8:28

Negotiating comes natural to me. It's like a second nature. I've never had to concentrate on it to be successful at it, especially when I know that I'm creating a win-win situation for me and my client. I think I first realized that I had a gift for it down in Miami. I was only 16, but I was able to convince my white boss to find jobs for those thirty-nine boys I had to leave behind at the work camp in Delray Beach.

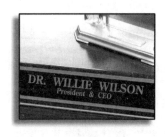 I love a profitable business day; a day where pending deals magically fall into place; a day where a new client is readily added to the books. That's the kind of day I recently had in St. Louis. We had two major appointments set for that day, so this called for a road trip from Chicago. I prefer driving if I can, because airplane schedules are too rigid. There's nothing worse than worrying about your departure time when you're in the middle of a productive conversation. Driving gives me the flexibility to nurture a client relationship. When I'm with them, they have my full attention for as long as it's needed.

On this particular trip, we were scheduled to hit the road at 3:30 am. That's not too early for me, but I don't think the employees who traveled with me felt exactly the same way. They arrived in the dark and we were off before dawn. As the sun rose, so did my spirit, and I looked forward to a good day.

The first appointment was with one of our major, established clients. Our purpose was mainly to spend some all-important "face time." In other words, a personal follow-up on some pending business. Face-to-face meetings like this reassures your clients of their continuing importance to you.

While we were there, I presented this client with a new idea regarding China that would globalize our partnership. I didn't plan to talk to them about this when we started out, but it came to me during our discussion, because my mind is constantly busy weighing opportunities and when I see one, I grab it. When it feels right, it feels good.

Our second appointment was with a new prospect. This is the type of meeting that really gets my adrenaline going. Here we are, the underdogs, a one hundred percent minority-owned company with a God-given opportunity to compete with the big guys. It is my goal to prove that we can do just that, and do it successfully. Integrity is the key. There is no substitute for it in the world of winning negotiations.

We closed the deal with that new prospect in just one hour, on our first call. Our success was partly due to my preliminary contact with the CEO, but a great deal of credit goes to an impeccable presentation by my VP/Director of Sales.

I think we may have come as a surprise to them, because this prospect came into the meeting prepared to make us part of their special diversity program. Nowadays, most major firms offer special programs to minority companies as a way of extending the proverbial helping hand. I am not snubbing my nose at those programs, and I do want to believe that they are helpful to many. However, I believe that our philosophy of hard work, our commitment, our integrity and our track record made that prospect-and any other large company we sit down with-realize that we're already competing on their level.

We returned to Chicago with a great sense of accomplishment and success, but it's not just about closing the deal. It's about my employees and the communities I serve. These are the things that are important in my life.

My cup runneth over.
Psalms 23:5

When I stop and think about it, I realize that I am happier than I have ever been in my life: I have a happy marriage, a thriving business and a fulfilling ministry. Everything my heart has ever desired, I have been given. Although it may not have come exactly when I wanted it, it has come to me.

My life has settled into a pleasing rhythm. I can face every day with joy because I am focused on Christ and I begin and end each day on my knees. I wake up early, around 4:00 AM. I can do that because I keep country hours, meaning I go to bed early. Very rarely will you find me up past midnight. So I rise before the sun and I spend a few hours meditating or reading Scripture. I fix my own breakfast. It's something light because I'm trying to stay healthy since cancer gave me that wake-up call. I don't rush into work because it can pretty much run without me now. Dale is my right arm, and I've been grooming Terrell to take more and more responsibility. I want him to learn everything there is to know about this business so that he can step into my shoes and not miss a beat when I retire.

Even then, I will not stop working. I will stay in the service of my ministry until the Lord calls me home.

**Your Father knoweth what things ye have need of
before ye ask Him.**
Matthew 6:8

If you asked me, "Wilson, if you could live your life over again, would you do things differently?" My answer would be "no." I would tell you to bring me this exact same way because all that I have gone through, all my hardships and trials, brought me to Christ. If I had had it easy, I would probably never have found Him. It's like that pearl in the oyster. It is the result of the oyster's hard times. My life is a string of pearls.

What shall I do next? Good question. I will wait upon the Lord to tell me. None of us knows what tomorrow will bring, but I don't have to worry since I found Jesus Christ. He is already into tomorrow ahead of me, paving my way to eternal life, and I find no fault in Him.

For though I be free from all men, yet have I made myself servant unto all, that I might gain the more.

I Corinthians 9:19

Biography of Dr. Willie Wilson

Within just four short decades, this African American product of the cotton and sugar cane fields of Louisiana, has managed to create a most impressive multi-million dollar empire, in spite of some of the most insurmountable obstacles one can imagine.

At age thirteen, with only twenty-five cents in his pocket, but big dreams in his head, Wilson left his sharecropper parents and ten siblings for a better life. In spite of being penniless and stranded numerous times, he now personally donates hundreds of thousands of dollars each year to small churches and community programs across the United States. In spite of being fired from numerous jobs, he went on to become owner of five

McDonald's restaurants within two and a half years; founder and producer of the first nationally syndicated African American gospel entertainment program on commercial television, now in its 20th year; and founder and CEO of one of America's fastest growing international medical supply companies. In spite of failed relationships; a son murdered in gang violence; and prostate cancer, today he enjoys a positive lifestyle with a fruitful marriage; and family members who help make up his dynasty.

Over the years, Wilson has received numerous awards including the Outstanding Store Award and Top Sales Performer Award for his hard work. He is the recipient of five honorary doctorate degrees.

In 1987, he founded Willie Wilson Productions: a television productions company where he produced the first nationally syndicated Gospel Entertainment Show ever seen on network television. The show, "Singsation" is seen today in over 40 million homes around the world. By the end of 1997, Wilson had sold his McDonald's restaurants and founded Omar Medical Supplies Inc. Through both of these successful companies, many needy individuals are supported. He gives generously to Churches and countless underprivileged neighborhoods.

After singing with the legendary Norfleet Brothers, Wilson produced five recordings: I'm So Grateful, Lord

Don't Let Me Fail, Just A Closer Walk With Thee, Through It All and I'll Fly Away. His latest, I'll Fly Away is distributed by Universal and is available in stores throughout the United States.

Wilson, who has lived in the Chicago area since 1965, resides with his wife of twelve years. He is the father of four grown children.

9